big stitch
QUILTING

"You can't use up creativity. The more you use, the more you have."

Maya Angelou, 1928–2014

big stitch
QUILTING

A practical guide to sewing
and hand quilting 20
stunning projects

CAROLYN FORSTER

SEARCH PRESS

First published in 2021

Search Press Limited
Wellwood, North Farm Road,
Tunbridge Wells, Kent TN2 3DR

Reprinted 2022

Text copyright © Carolyn Forster 2021

Photographs by Mark Davison
Styling by Lisa Brown
Photographs and design copyright
© Search Press Ltd 2021

ISBN: 978-1-78221-821-0
ebook ISBN: 978-1-78126-788-2

The Publishers and author can accept no responsibility
for any consequences arising from the information,
advice or instructions given in this publication.

Readers are permitted to reproduce any of the items/
patterns in this book for their personal use, or for the
purposes of selling for charity, free of charge and without
the prior permission of the Publishers. Any use of the
items/patterns for commercial purposes is not permitted
without the prior permission of the Publishers.

Suppliers
For details of suppliers, please visit the Search Press
website: www.searchpress.com.

The projects in this book have been made using imperial
measurements, and the metric equivalents provided
have been calculated following standard conversion
practices. The metric measurements are often rounded
to the nearest .25mm for ease of use except in rare
circumstances; however, if you need more exact
measurements, there are a number of excellent online
converters that you can use. Always use either metric or
imperial measurements, not a combination of both.

Publisher's note
All the step-by-step photographs in this book feature the
author, Carolyn Forster.

Acknowledgements

With grateful thanks to the ever-
wonderful team at Search Press,
who manage to make sense of my
ramblings and continue to produce
beautiful books for the crafting world.

Many thanks to Helen Ott, for kindly
lending me pieces from her inspiring
Japanese textile collection, featured
on pages 11 and 13.

CONTENTS

When I first started making patchwork quilts, there were very few books giving information on the process, and a far smaller selection of waddings/battings and patchwork fabrics available. I quilted one of my first quilts with cotton stranded embroidery thread/floss and a big embroidery needle, as that was the only thing that would work on the thick polyester wadding/batting and fabric combinations that I had used. These bold stitches held the layers together perfectly, adding texture and colour at the same time. When I met with other quilters, I soon saw that in order to conform with what was expected of a quilter and a quilted piece at that time I really needed to be making small stitches and more intricate quilting designs.

Eventually, I had made enough of these 'small-stitch' quilts of heirloom quality to be asked to teach others. I loved having the chance to share my passion with others but soon realized that it was often hard for new quilters to make the small stitches, and it wasn't always easy for them to thread the small needles. It made me think back to my early quilting days, and about those big stitches and larger needles. Surely other quilters must have quilted like that, too?

The more research I did into quilting designs and methods, the more eye-opening the world of past quilts and quilting became. There were many quilts that had not achieved the museum status of the intricately quilted, heirloom-quality pieces that we had thought we ought to aspire to. These quilts were often referred to as 'utility quilts', and when discovered in people's homes, were often in a sorry state due to the sheer amount of use and love they had endured over the years. These quilts would often wear out and fall apart, and then sometimes pieces would be reused to make up new patchwork quilts. Gradually, more used and worn quilts came to light due to quilt documentation days held by quilting guilds.

Quilt historians and those interested in social history pounced upon the chance to find out all they could about these quilts, studying the fabrics, construction methods and the quilting styles and threads. This opened up a whole new world of quilting: bigger stitches, thicker threads and bold quilting designs, there to get the job done efficiently and quickly – and to get the quilt on the bed and into use.

So with this information, and many examples to lead the way, I started teaching quilters that there were other ways to quilt. Yes, it was fine to use thicker threads and big stitches, bold designs, and to not spend forever trying to hand quilt a quilt. Yes, you can still aspire to fine handwork, and you can use big stitch quilting as a starting point.

With the growing popularity of big stitch, there are now many resources and pieces of work to study. Here, I have included stitches such as Mennonite Tacks, Methodist Knots and Running Cross Stitch – all stitches used in the past to make the process of making a quilt quick, easy and enjoyable. I have used quilting motifs that are often simple in their design and quick to stitch, allowing the quilts to show off the fabrics.

WHAT IS
big stitch
QUILTING?

We are all familiar with quilting – the running stitches that hold the layers of a quilt together – but mostly we associate this with fine, small stitches. Big stitch quilting still holds the three layers of a quilt together, but is bolder in its finished look, and faster to sew. It is something we find in quilting for as long as quilts have existed. Look at collections in museums and you will see beautifully executed stitches and ornate designs, but you will also find quilts that have simpler designs and often bigger stitches and thicker threads. The quilting on these quilts is not fussy and fancy or ornate. It is often functional rather than ornamental.

Using these big stitches and bold threads is sometimes termed 'utility quilting'. Utilities are often seen as the basics we need to keep us going: think of your gas, water and electricity. Looking for further definitions of the word *utility*, I found that in economics the word is used to describe a measure of relative satisfaction. And we can use this word in that sense when applied to our quilting. Many quilters still enjoy the process of hand quilting – it gives them a level of real satisfaction – they just sometimes need it to be simpler and quicker in this modern day.

Quilts held together with basic stitching and using simple designs can be found all over the world, from Wagga Wagga in Australia, boromono in Japan, kantha in Bangladesh, Amish and Gee's Bend quilts in America to stripy quilts from northern England. We'll explore these in more detail over the following few pages. Taking inspiration from our forebears and from around the world, many of the quilts and projects in this book draw on different cultural and historical sources, often blending and overlapping them.

HISTORICAL AND CULTURAL EXAMPLES OF BIG STITCH-STYLE QUILTING

When I first quilted with stranded embroidery thread/floss and a big needle, little did I realize that so many quilt makers before me, from all around the world, had been in that same position. They knew what I was learning: that big, visible stitches were there to do a job, and can be beautiful too.

Utility quilts and the Great Depression

During times of hardship it becomes necessary to use what you have. And if what you have is a quilt pieced from heavyweight fabrics, then fine thread and fine stitches are not going to do the job. As big stitch quilting is a bolder style of quilting and the designs are usually more widely spaced, less thread is required. In some Depression era (1930s) quilts, the thick quilting thread used was thought to be the sewing thread that had been used to hold flour or feedsacks together, which themselves were unpicked and sewn into quilts. Using a bigger stitch to quilt the quilts was another way to get the job done faster, when sack quilts provided one of the only affordable ways of keeping warm at night.

Gee's Bend quilts

These quilts are associated with the African American community of Gee's Bend (offically known as Boykin), Wilcox County, Alabama, USA. These wonderful, colourful quilts were made by the women in this isolated community and have a freedom and style all of their own, likened by some to modern art. This joyful creativity continues today, both with the style of quilting and the size of the stitches and threads used. Looking at the style of stitching has opened the eyes of many quilt makers and allowed them to free up their ideas in their own quilts.

Australian Wagga Wagga quilts

These quilts, named after a town in Australia, are the classic utility quilt of Australia – often stitched from fabric rectangles and squares. Frugally made from what was to hand, they were then quilted with coarse thread and large stitches to get them into use quickly. This is a style of quilt and quilting born of necessity during trying circumstances.

Japanese boromono (or boro) quilts and sashiko stitching

Many of us are perhaps familiar with the indigo fabric and the white even stitches of sashiko. The precise way the designs are stitched and the wonderful patterns make this a distinctive form of stitching. As well as being seen on small household textiles, the stitching can also be found on old clothing, when layers needed to be built up and held together to keep out the cold. Chiku chiku has become a popular and accessible style of Japanese big stitch quilting.

Less well known are the boromono pieces of cloth or clothing that were made from discarded rags and old clothing, held together with sashiko-style stitching. Quilts of this style were stitched with a coarser thread and stitch technique, often due to circumstance (for example, poor lighting and old thread). This was not stitching for show, but for necessity. Boromono has now become very sought after, and is often hung as an art form. Less control and more freedom can be seen in this form of Japanese stitching, and it is often easier for a beginner to access on their indigo and white stitching journey.

Opposite: English North Country quilt from the 1930s. The heavy wadding/batting and cotton sateen outer is quilted with a strong thick thread to hold the heavy layers together.

Above and right: vintage Japanese textile pieces, illustrating how stitches were used in a utilitarian way to patch and continue the use of household textiles.

Indian kantha, Siddi and godhadi quilts

Throughout the huge country of India there are many diverse peoples whose textile practices have developed over many years and with different cultural influences.

Kantha is often viewed as the classic Indian quilt, but there are many variations of it, and blurrings of techniques and styles. Kantha are made in Bangladesh and the eastern states of India. They are made from layered saris and stitched together with a running stitch. They are often colourful due to the use of sari fabric, and can be patched to make the cloth to the desired size. Kantha can also be highly decorative and embroidery-like, with running stitches in many colours making pictures on a neutral cloth. These images are then surrounded by running stitches in a neutral thread, which acts as a background.

Godhadi quilts are riotous in colour and come from the areas of Goa and Maharashtra. They are made of many fabrics, including sari, but often have more patchwork. They are made of more layers than kantha, often as many as six, but contain no wadding/batting layer, so are heavier. The quilting has more direction than the straight lines of kantha, often containing circles and swirls.

Siddi or kawandi quilts come from the western part of India, below Pakistan, and are made by people of African descent who came to India through enslavement by the Portuguese in the sixteenth century. One of their traditions is the making of bed quilts, locally known as kawandi, to be slept on in the hot weather, or under in the cooler monsoon season. They have a sari base and appliquéd patches of fabric built up on top, from a corner or the centre. These patches are held down with running stitch, and the layers of overlapping patches are built up to cover the base cloth. Traditionally they are finished with a folded fabric square at each corner, known as a *phula* or 'flower', and some consider the kawandi unfinished without these.

Above and left: two different styles of Indian kantha, showing the running stitches securing the layers of cloth together.

Visible mending and mindfulness

Mending and repairing clothes and textile items has been seen in the recent past as a job only necessary if you could not afford to replace old for new. However, with the resurgence of repairing being recognized as great for the recycling of textiles and clothes, and a reduction of waste, this kind of stitching has taken on a greater importance. In some cases, it can be seen as an art form.

If you are going to create a repair then make it a feature – the time taken on this is viewed as something to savour. The whole idea of stitching as meditation has also become very popular – anyone who has hand stitched knows how valuable those moments of calm with oneself can be. With the simple running stitch the mainstay of much textile repair, it is easy to see how this kind of work can become desirable.

Wabi-sabi

This Japanese aesthetic celebrates the imperfect. The term is used to describe an ethos or feeling around the broken or worn, and the processes used to make an item useful or functional once more. Textiles repaired for reuse with stitches that are visible, where the maker is not ashamed of the textile's past, is a common theme. It fits well with the idea of repair, reuse and recycle, which has often been the inspiration point for many types of big stitch projects and quilts.

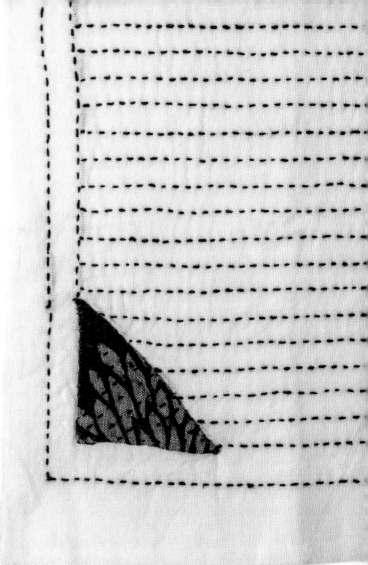

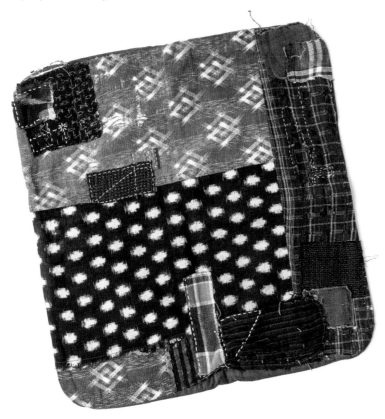

Above: a Japanese tray cloth stitched with a simple running or sashiko stitch and a feature made of the fabric triangle.

Left: a small Japanese household item patched over time, with visible stitching.

TOOLS & MATERIALS

NEEDLES

Generally, the needles you will need for big stitch quilting will be larger than those used for general sewing, in order to accommodate a thicker thread and to make the stitching process comfortable. Depending on the thread that is used, the needles you work with will vary. Having a selection to hand will give you the most flexibility with your quilting. What is important, though, is that the needle makes a hole in the fabric that is wide enough for the thread to go through comfortably. You should not have to tug unnecessarily.

Try to choose from a quality brand, as the production and finishing methods vary for needles, and it is worth paying a bit more for something that will be a pleasure to work with. When it comes to size, there is no real rule; you are trying to find a needle that is comfortable for you to work with. A good selection might include:

- Chenille, sizes 22 and 24
- Betweens, sizes 3 to 6
- Embroidery, size 6
- Sashiko, mixed sizes.

Note

When threading a needle, I always find it easier to hold the thread and put the needle over it, rather than trying to poke the thread through the needle's eye. If you find threading the needle difficult, invest in a needle threader, or easy-thread needles.

THIMBLES

When I quilt I use a thimble with a ridge around its top on the finger which is underneath the work; I find that the ridge helps me make the stitches as I push the needle against it. On the hand above the work I wear a metal dimpled thimble to push the needle along. There are lots of thimbles and finger protectors to try, and it may take a while, and some patience, to find the ones that best work for you.

Although I try to use a combination of needle and thread that are smooth to work with, occasionally I find I need an extra tug to get the thread through the layers. Try using a needle grabber, or the side of a silicone thimble, to add extra grip.

THREADS

The threads that can be used for big stitch quilting stitches are generally thicker than regular quilting thread, which is often 28wt, and there is a wide selection to choose from. The lower the weight number, the thicker the thread will be. You will be looking at threads that say 16wt, 12wt or even 8wt on the label, but different brands can vary in the actual thickness, and so will the type of thread used. The thread that you choose may vary from project to project depending on the stitches used and the look that you want for your quilt. You will no doubt end up with favourites.

Below is a selection that offers a wide choice of colour and texture. Consider using variegated threads, too, for extra interest.

- Valdani no. 12 perle cotton
- Aurifil no. 12
- Coton à broder no. 16
- Crochet cotton
- Wonderfil Spaghetti no. 12
- Sashiko thread.

A selection of threads, needles, thimbles and needle grabbers ideal for use for big stitch quilting.

Rotary cutter

Like a pizza wheel, a rotary cutter cuts through up to about eight layers of fabric at a time. Keep the blade sharp and free of nicks, and cut through as many or as few layers as you are comfortable with.

Self-healing cutting mat

This is a purpose-made mat, available from craft stores, on which to cut your fabric using the rulers and cutters. It is marked into a grid that you can use to help you measure and cut the fabric in straight lines. Buy the largest size you can afford, as the larger the cutting mat, the less you will need to fold your fabric.

OTHER KEY EQUIPMENT

Pins

Long, fine pins with a glass head are the most useful for keeping fabrics in place before stitching.

Quilter's tape measure

This type of tape measure is longer than normal and so is useful for measuring bed lengths and quilt sides. It is 120in (300cm) long.

Template plastic

This is a sturdy but thin plastic that can be drawn on or traced through and then cut with normal scissors. To write on the plastic, you should use a fine permanent marker pen.

Iron

Your patchwork will need pressing, so a good hot iron is useful. You can use a steam iron, but be careful not to distort the seams when pressing.

Hera marker

This is a useful tool for creasing seams and marking quilting designs (see also page 31).

Chalk marker

This marker is used like a pen and leaves a thin white line on the fabric that brushes off easily. It is ideal for marking on patterns and stitch lines.

CUTTING EQUIPMENT

Scissors

Use a large pair of long-bladed scissors for cutting the fabrics. I have a specialist pair of quilting scissors that is ideal for this purpose. Small scissors with fine points make snipping threads easy and give you more control over the blades.

Quick unpick

Use this tool to undo sewing mistakes quickly and easily. I also use the point to help guide in the fabric under the machine foot, close to the needle, which helps to protect my fingers.

Rulers

Various specialist acrylic rulers are available that work with a rotary cutter and self-healing cutting mat to cut the fabric easily and quickly in layers where necessary. The various types that you could use for the projects in this book are described with the relevant project instructions.

FABRIC

Because of the wide range of influences on the big stitch style of quilted projects and quilts, there is a large pool of fabric combinations to dip into. Many of the past makers used fabrics they had to hand, or were trying to make something that was worn out last just a little bit longer. Whichever way you choose to select the fabrics for the quilts and projects, make sure they are clean and pressed for easier working. It is also important that you enjoy working with them, and if something is making the job hard, set it aside and pick different fabrics that are pleasing in your hand. Depending on the project, fabrics with wear and tear can actually enhance the finished piece, as the need to repair them or use what is left can enhance the creative process. Using fabrics from your past or with family significance can make the final result more meaningful, and sometimes therapeutic to work with. Try to use fabrics that can show off the stitches rather than hiding them away.

BACKING FABRIC

Choose a fabric that is a similar weight to that used on the front of the quilt; you will want a fabric that will be easy to work with and nice to handle. The backing can be a patterned or plain fabric. If you choose plain, remember that your quilting stitches will be highly visible, whereas a patterned fabric will hide them – not, perhaps, what you might want after hours of careful hand quilting.

The backing fabric will need to be wider and longer than the patchwork top in order to accommodate the shrinkage or 'pulling up' of the quilt top and the wadding/batting when you quilt. The surplus fabric (and wadding/batting) will be trimmed off when you come to bind the quilt.

WADDING

Wadding (also known as batting) is the soft filling that goes between the patchwork top and the backing fabric. It can be made from polyester, cotton (or a combination of both), wool, and even recycled plastic bottles or sustainably grown bamboo. The important things to think about are how much quilting you want to do and how 'puffy' you want the quilt to be. This 'puffiness' is called 'loft' and it gives the quilt its characteristic look.

All wadding/batting states on the packaging how far apart you can space the quilting. If you do not want to do too much quilting, then one that recommends quilting up to 10in (25.5cm) apart would be a good choice. For denser quilting, choose a wadding/batting that needs quilting every 2–4in (5–10cm). Ask other quilters what they use, and they might give you an off-cut that you can try out before buying.

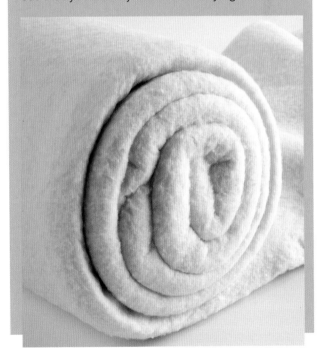

QUILT HOOP

For large quilts, i.e. anything bigger than a pillow cover, I use a hoop. They are generally wooden and round, and the most common and useful size is a 14in (35.5cm) round. The quilt should be flat and loosely held in the hoop so that you can use both hands for the quilting. When I work, the hand under the quilt, wearing a ridged thimble, pushes the quilt layers up to make a 'hill', which the needle will push against to make the stitch.

STITCHING the PATCHWORK

Here are some hints and tips to help you when stitching your patchwork on the sewing machine.

BEFORE YOU BEGIN

Read through all the instructions before you start on a project. Make sure you have all the materials and equipment you need, and that you are familiar with the techniques used. For the projects in this book:

- All seam allowances (SA) are ¼in (5mm) unless otherwise stated
- All fabric cut off the bolt is cut across the width, unless otherwise stated
- All fabric quantities are based on a 42in (106.5cm) useable width of fabric (WoF)
- WS means wrong side of the fabric; RS means right side.

STITCH LENGTH

When machine stitching, set your straight-stitch length to 11 or 2.0 to 2.5, depending on how your machine is calibrated. It needs to be small enough to hold the fabrics together, but large enough to unpick easily, if the need arises.

When you are sewing fabric pieces together that will then be cut and re-sewn (see pages 20–21), you may want to set the stitch length a little smaller than usual so that the stitches do not come undone easily when they are cut through.

PRESSING

This is done with a hot iron and a pressing pad or ironing board. Whether you use steam or not is up to you; some people think it distorts the work, but this hasn't been my experience.

I do press my work from the front and not from the back. I find that by doing this I eliminate the little pleats that often occur when you press from the back, which then have to be removed by pressing from the front, making the process twice as long!

Take care to position the work and the seam you want to press correctly; you will then find you can press in one stroke.

FINGER PRESSING

Finger pressing (shown below) involves squeezing the fabric between your finger and thumb and is a quick method of marking the fabric. It leaves a semi-permanent crease and is a more accurate way of marking than pinning. It also eliminates the need to put in a pin that will then immediately need to be removed.

Finger pressing

CHAIN PIECING

This method of joining fabric pieces involves continuously feeding pairs of fabric pieces in under the machine foot, one after the other, with a gap of about ⅜in (1cm) between them. The pieces are held together by the sewing thread, hence the term 'chain piecing'. The advantage of this method is that it saves on thread when you have to sew lots of patches together in pairs.

1 Lay two fabric pieces together, RS facing, and stitch along the seam. When you reach the end, position the next pair of fabric pieces ready for stitching, leaving a gap of about ⅜in (1cm). Stitch across the gap and then along the next seam.

2 When you have stitched all the fabric pieces, simply snip through the threads joining them together.

SEW-THEN-CUT TECHNIQUE

Most of the time in patchwork we cut the shapes out and then sew them back together to get our desired pattern or look. However, sometimes it is quicker, more efficient and more accurate to sew fabrics together, cut them up and then sew again. This means we sew larger pieces first and have fewer small fiddly pieces. For this example I have used two 10in (26cm) squares in different fabrics.

Note

It is best for this technique to have your machine sew with a smaller stitch than usual. This will stop the stitches unravelling when you cut through a sewn line.

1 Lay one 10in (26cm) square on top of another, RS together.

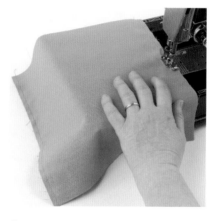

2 Stitch a seam down two opposite sides.

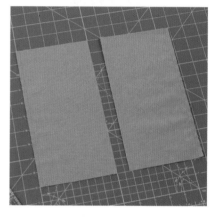

3 Cut the stitched squares through the centre (the pieces will now measure 5in/13cm wide).

4 Sew again along the long open edge of each piece, then cut each rectangle into two through the centre.

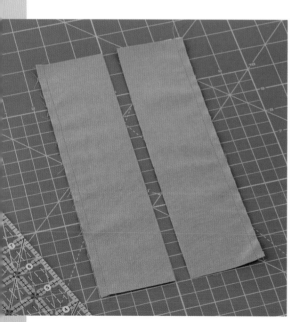

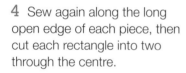

5 Press the seams towards the same fabric on each piece; here it is the floral fabric.

6 Place the two pieces right sides together, so that the top green piece sits on top of the lower floral piece, and sew together along one side edge.

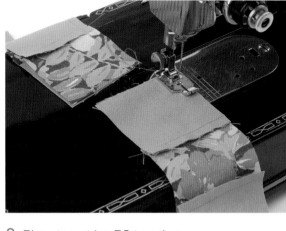

7 Open out and press the seams towards the floral fabric again. Cut the square into four equal four-patch strips (they will each measure 2½in/6.5cm wide). Arrange them in a checkerboard pattern, as shown.

8 Place two strips RS together, again matching upper greens with lower florals; chain piece to sew the strips together (see page 19). Because of the way you pressed your strips, the seams will knit together (see note, below).

9 Press the seams open this time.

10 Place the two pieces RS together, again matching upper greens with lower florals. Sew the two pieces together then open out the seam and press open.

The finished block.

Note

Pressing the seams in the same direction in the early stages means that they will 'knit together' neatly, preventing all the bulk in one place when you sew them together later.

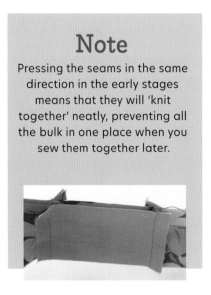

TACKING/BASTING

PREPARING TO QUILT

In preparation for layering and tacking (also known as basting) the quilt, press the quilt top and backing fabric. If you can, leave them somewhere flat so that they will not need a second pressing (draped over a spare bed or stair rail is ideal). Unfold the wadding/batting the day before, to allow it to relax so that any creases can fall out. If you leave the wadding/batting in a steamy bathroom overnight this works well, or, if you run out of time, put the wadding/batting in the tumble dryer on the refresh cycle and this will do the same job!

Holding the layers together

By trying the different methods on the following pages, you will find one that suits you and your quilt; often this will depend on the quilt in question.

Generally for all methods of tacking/basting (except using spray glue) the securing method should form a grid, often dictated by the patches in the quilt (see page 25). There should not usually be a gap bigger than 6in (15cm) between the tacking/basting – about the size of your spread hand. If the patchwork does not have a grid to follow, use your hand span as a ready guide.

Think about the way that the quilt will be quilted before you tack/baste it. Depending on the way that you quilt, you may not even need to tack/baste the layers together. For example, if you use a stand-up traditional frame with rollers, this will eliminate the tacking/basting process completely. Consider this option if you have the space at home and enjoy hand quilting in one particular place, as these are not easy to shift from one room to another!

If you use a circular hoop then safety-pin tacking/basting (see page 24) might not be the best choice. This is because the pins tend to get in the way of the hoop and need moving every time you reposition the hoop. If you are happy to keep doing this, then go ahead! It bothers some people but not others, so it is worth being aware before you start.

When you lap quilt, you do not have the additional stability that a hoop gives the work, so a little denser tacking/basting will help to stop the layers shifting. For lap quilting, think about tacking/basting perhaps every 4in (10cm) rather than 6in (15cm). Use your closed fist as a gauge between tacking/basting lines, rather than a spread hand.

HAND TACKING

Traditionally hand tacking/basting a quilt together may not be your idea of a quick method, but depending on where you do it and how many people are involved it might be worth considering. Hand tacking/basting a quilt does, I think, give you the best control over the layers of the quilt and does not add any extra weight or bulk. Another reason I like to hand tack/baste is that it gives me time to really look at the quilt. I can spend time thinking about how it might best be quilted. When I am stitching a quilt I do not always give thought to how it will be quilted – the tacking/basting process gives me that time.

- Use a flat, clear floor – community and church halls have this space, so book the space when you know the cleaner has just been! This saves you having to move your own furniture around to make room for the quilt on the floor. Secure the edges with masking tape; if you're using a carpeted floor, the quilt will not move around as much as on a smooth floor.
- For any tacking/basting done on the floor, consider using a kneeling mat or knee pads to protect your knees during the process. If this isn't an option, try to use a large table.
- Tack/baste a quilt with a group of friends – take it in turns to help each other out.
- If a group near you has a frame for tacking/basting, check to see if they will hire it out, or if they offer a service to tack/baste quilts.
- Use the services of a long-arm quilter. Many offer a tacking/basting service, which lets you sit down and enjoy the quilting. This thread-tacked/basted method offers all the advantages of manageability and no added weight, but with someone else having done the work!

How to hand tack

- Use specialist tacking/basting thread, as this breaks easily and is cheaper that regular sewing thread. Start with a knot and a backstitch.
- Work the stitch from right to left on the quilt (left to right if you are left-handed).
- The stitches should be about ½in (1cm) long and evenly spaced (see diagram below).
- Finish with a backstitch to keep the thread secure.
- To help ease the needle up through the layers, use a teaspoon (see page 28, showing the use with a safety pin). As the needle and your hands are always on the top of the quilt, your fingers can get sore as the needle pushes up against them; pushing the needle up against the edge of a teaspoon makes the process quicker.

Tailor's tacking

Some people find the action of tacking/basting uncomfortable, as the needle is held horizontal to your body. If this is the case, try tailor's tacking, or diagonal tacking, where the needle is held so it points at your body, which is sometimes a more natural action. When using this stitch, it is often enough to tack/baste the quilt in rows 6in (15cm) apart and not create a grid.

- Thread the needle with tacking/basting thread and knot the end. Work the stitch from right to left on the quilt (left to right if you are left-handed). Create rows of ½–1in (1–2.5cm) long diagonal stitches, depending on the length of the needle. Finish with a backstitch.

ALTERNATIVES TO HAND TACKING/BASTING

Sometimes there are things that stand in the way of us hand tacking/basting a quilt comfortably and quickly. If you don't want to do all that tacking/basting, which, after all, will just be taken out when it's done the job, then consider safety pins, tacking guns and spray-baste glue. Combine these methods of tacking/basting with table-top tacking/basting for maximum efficiency!

Tacking/basting gun

A tacking/basting gun is a good alternative method (see image, below). Tack/baste every 3–4in (7.5–10cm), with a basting grate slipped underneath the quilt sandwich. If you don't have a basting grate, use a wire cooling rack. Keep moving the grate and tacking/basting the layers together. Once the quilt is covered, tack/baste around the edge. When it comes to removing the tacks, either use a tool designed for the job or a curved pair of scissors if you have some. In either case, try not to snip the quilt fabric! If you are worried about this, snip the tacks from the back of the quilt, as the damage will be less noticeable there than on the front!

Spray glue

Use a reliable spray such as 505 Spray & Fix. Follow the product instructions and work on the quilt in sections.

Fusible wadding/batting

For smaller projects, consider using the iron-on waddings/battings that are available. Start on small quilts until you gain some experience.

Safety pins

Safety pins are a great, fast way to get a quilt tacked/basted (see the pink and yellow versions, above). Working from the top of the quilt, insert the pin and bring it back up through all three layers. Bring the point of the pin up against the edge of a teaspoon (see page 28) and clip the pin closed. Some people find the pins with pin covers easier on the hands – they give you something bigger to get hold of, and 'magically' the open pins do not stick together in clumps when stored, so it is quick and easy to pull out one pin at a time.

The pins should be spaced neither too densely nor too sparsely. If you can spread your hand on the quilt and just touch the pins, that is a good density. When the quilt is covered with pins, tack/baste around the edge as for hand tacking/basting.

TACKING THE LAYERS TOGETHER

When tacking/basting a quilt, I find it easiest to keep to a grid system. As I always use the same system, I don't have to think or plan, I just tack/baste! I tack/baste the quilts on a carpeted floor, which helps to keep the layers from shifting. If you have smooth floors, be aware that they may need protection, in case the needle catches as it goes through the fabric. Either protect the floor by using a rotary cutter mat between the backing and the floor, moving it as you tack/baste, or perhaps consider table tacking/basting (see pages 26–28).

System of tacking/basting

This is the way I hand tack/baste my quilts when they are on the floor. It smooths out wrinkles and flattens any puffs that may arise. Tools to make it quicker or more comfortable include thimbles, spoons, masking tape, needles and a kneeling mat or knee pads.

1 Press the backing fabric and lay it on the floor WS upwards. Pat it gently flat. Secure to the floor with tabs of masking tape at the corners and the mid-points on all four sides. Do NOT stretch the fabric. If you stretch the fabric, it will retract back to its natural position when the masking tape comes off and the backing that is, by then, tacked/basted together in the quilt will start to pucker. We do not want that!

2 Lay the wadding/batting on top of the backing fabric. If it helps, fold the wadding/batting into four and line up the outside edge with the corner of the backing fabric then unfold a quarter at a time. This way, the middles of the backing and wadding/batting are central and you don't spend time re-adjusting the layers. Pat flat.

3 Press the patchwork top for the last time. Now place the patchwork on top of the wadding/batting, RS up. Again fold into quarters if this helps. As your backing and wadding/batting will usually be slightly larger than your quilt top you will be left with a margin all the way around. Pat flat. Add some tabs of masking tape at the corners.

4 Pin the three layers together in the centre, at the corners and the mid-point on each side. This is just to keep things in place while you tack/baste.

5 If you are hand tacking/basting, start with a knot and a backstitch to secure your thead. Start by tacking/basting the diagonals (a). If sewing, use a teaspoon to bring the needle up out of the quilt for ease, or use your thimble to protect your fingers. Finish with a backstitch. You never need to have your hand under the quilt; you are working from the top all of the time. This way you do not disturb the layers.

6 Tack/baste across the middle in both directions (b). Remove the pins as you come across them.

7 Using your hand span as a guide, tack/baste in rows from the centre, working towards the outside edge (c). When this section is full, move round to the next (d). There are four sections to fill in this way, always starting from the middle and working towards the outside edge (e and f).

8 When complete, tack/baste ¼in (5mm) away from the outside edge of the quilt sandwich. This will eventually be removed, as the quilt gradually shifts when you quilt it, but in the meantime will stop the edges getting tatty or stretched.

9 Remove the masking tape, and pick up the quilt (and yourself) from the floor! If you like, you can now fold over the extra wadding/batting and backing fabric and tack/baste it abutting the edge of the quilt.

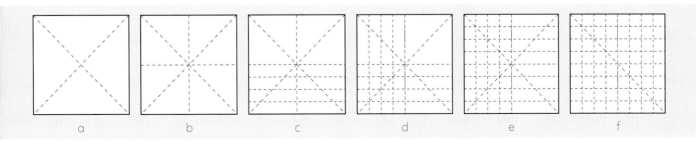

a   b   c   d   e   f

TABLE-TOP QUILT TACKING

Learning to tack/baste on a table top will save you crawling around on the floor, and often having to clear the space in the first place. It will mean that you can sit and work in relative comfort without the worry of sore knees or putting a room out of use while you use the floor space. The table does not have to be as big as the quilt – you can use a large dining table, ping pong table or wallpaper pasting table. I use a 24 x 31in (61 x 79cm) collapsible picnic table that folds away for easy storage.

You will need

- A table at a comfortable height for you to work at. I use a picnic table with a smooth surface. As I only use it for this, I don't have to worry about damaging it with pins. If you use a dining table, protect it with an oilcloth tablecloth, or slide a large cutting mat between the layered quilt and the table, and move this around as needed to protect the table from pins and needle marks.
- Chair: I use an office chair to sit on so that I can adjust the height
- Masking tape, cocktail sticks/toothpicks
- Clips or clamps, or bulldog clips

Method

1 Measure and mark the centre of the table with a cross, and mark the halfway points on each side of the table. Then, re-mark these positions by sticking a cocktail stick/tooth pick on top using masking tape. For the centre mark, stick one in place, then cut another in half, and stick down to the table. These will need to be removed before you actually tack/baste, but you need them initially to feel the centre of the table when the fabric and wadding/batting is positioned. Some people just put the sticks on the outside edge of the table, as they are easier to remove. After some practice you will see what works best for you.

2 Press the backing fabric and fold it into quarters, WS together. Place it on the table – the RS of the fabric will be facing you and, as you unfold it, the WS will be uppermost.

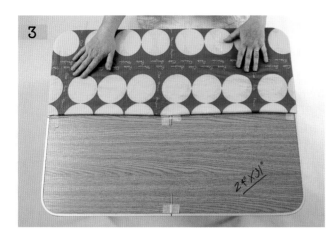

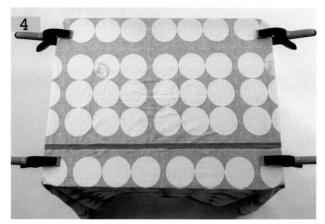

3 Unfold the backing fabric. Line up the edges with the points on the sides of the table so as to keep it straight.

4 Use the clips or clamps to secure the fabric to the edges of the table. If the quilt is smaller than the table, the edges that don't overhang can be taped into place. There is no need to stretch the fabric – it just needs to lay flat, and this is done by gently patting the fabric and securing in place with a clamp at each corner. If the fabric is stretched, when the clamps are undone, the fabric will release and make ripples.

5 Now fold the wadding/batting in the same way and place on top of the backing fabric. You can feel the cocktail stick markers through the backing fabric, so you can use these to ensure the wadding/batting is squared up and central on the backing. Smooth the wadding/batting by patting gently, without stretching it. Replace the clips already in position to hold both layers in place.

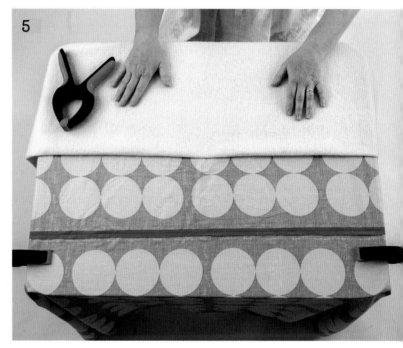

6 Press the quilt top and fold into quarters WS facing out. Match the centre of the top to the centre of the wadding/batting, and unfold as for the other layers. The quilt top will now be right side up (see step 7 on page 28).

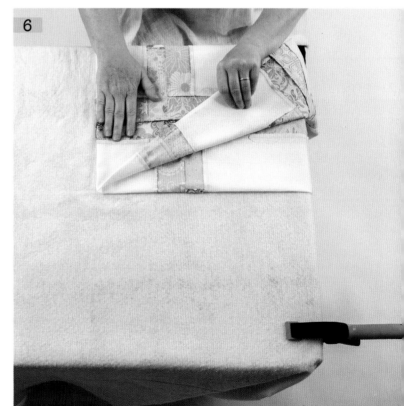

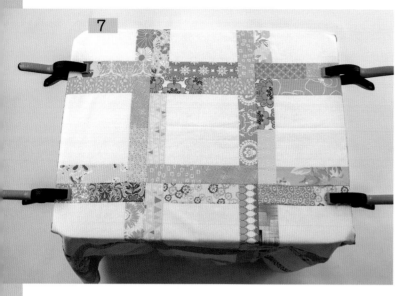

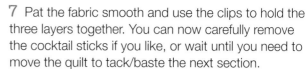

7 Pat the fabric smooth and use the clips to hold the three layers together. You can now carefully remove the cocktail sticks if you like, or wait until you need to move the quilt to tack/baste the next section.

8 Tack/baste the area that is being held on the table. One of the keys to tacking/basting with thread or safety pins is only working from the front of the quilt. If you find it hard to push the needle or the pin heads up from the table, use a teaspoon. Working from right to left (or left to right if you are left-handed), tack/baste in rows about 6in (15cm) apart.

9 When the area of the quilt on top of the table is complete, take off the clips (and tape if using) and shift the layers towards or away from you so the next untacked/unbasted area is on the table top.

10 Secure the side of the quilt that has been tacked/basted, then pat the backing flat and secure with clips. Make sure the wadding/batting is flat again on the backing and reposition the quilt top in place. Use tape if needed and replace the last two clamps. Tack/baste as before. Continue like this until the entire quilt is tacked/basted. You will need to move the quilt between three to nine times to completely tack/baste it. When this is complete, tack/baste ¼in (5mm) away from the outside edge all round the quilt top.

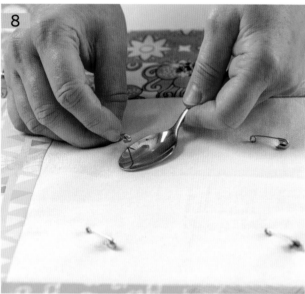

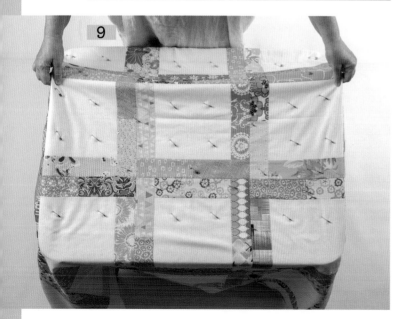

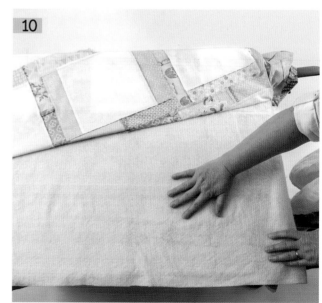

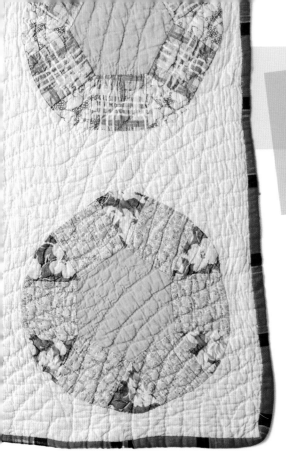

QUILT
designs

BAPTIST FAN, WAVE OR ELBOW QUILTING

This design goes by various names thanks to the many church groups and individuals who used the design frequently. These names include Amish Wave, Mennonite Fan, Baptist Fan and Wave. There may be different approaches to the size or the way the pattern is made, but they all have the same result. These designs need minimal marking, and generally can be quilted in one direction in an easy movement. They are a repeated pattern that can be sewn all over the quilt top, and generally do not take account of the patchwork.

Historically, they were designs quilted out of necessity: they were quick to quilt compared to elaborate feathers and wreaths, and the designs could be created from items that were common in most homes, such as cups, saucepan lids, and elbows for the really large waves. They were popular in quilts of the Depression era, and commonly used thicker threads to hold the layers together.

The design is quilted from the outside edge of the quilt working in towards the centre, or in rows from bottom to top. If a quilt was positioned in a square frame and being quilted by a group of people, one person could sit on each side and quilt the design, working in towards the centre of the quilt (like the quilting on the Fabric Stack quilt, see page 64). If you were quilting on a frame with rollers, you would quilt the design in rows starting at the bottom of the quilt, working towards the top as you rolled the next part of the quilt on (as on the Octagons quilt, see page 52).

This is a popular design for a number of reasons. The fan is quilted on the bias of the fabric, which seems to give more readily under the needle and so make it easier to quilt. The design covers the quilt all over, ignoring the piecing and so acts as a unifying feature. It can be stitched by any level of quilter and so is a good choice for a beginner. It can be quilted by groups around a frame, as the design can be worked from the outside edge inwards to the centre of the quilt. And although the design is mainly seen with single lines of quilting, it can also be worked with the lines of quilting in groups of two or three.

Amish Wave worked from the outside in.

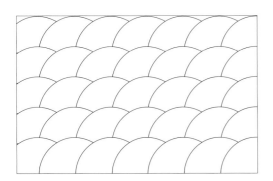

Amish Wave worked in rows from the bottom to the top.

MAKING A WAVE TEMPLATE

A template makes it easy to create even waves. You can use the one given on page 140, or make your own to any size you require by using either a compass or with any circular household object.

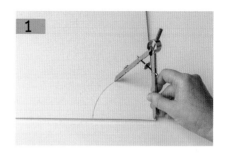

With a compass

1 Set the compass to the size of the arc you would like, and place it in the corner of a sheet of paper. Draw the quarter circle.

2 Now move the compass point to where the circle line touched the bottom edge of the paper and draw another arc from the paper edge up to meet the first arc. This second shape is the template for the quilting design. Either trace onto template plastic, or glue to card and cut out.

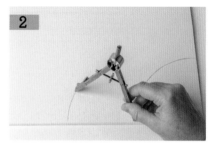

With a plate

1 Draw around a round object such as a plate, saucepan lid or pan onto a piece of paper.

2 Cut out the circle and fold into quarters.

3 Aligning the straight edges of the quarter-circle in the bottom right-hand corner of another sheet of card or template plastic, draw around the curve to create the first arc.

4 Unfold the paper to make a half circle and align with the bottom and right-hand edges of the paper. Draw around this shape, from the bottom left upwards, until the line of the second arc meets the line of the first arc.

5 Remove the paper circle, and cut out the second shape, which is the template for your fan quilting.

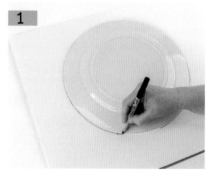

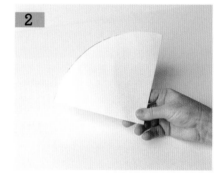

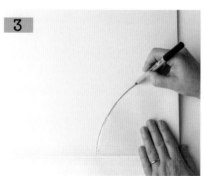

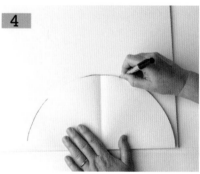

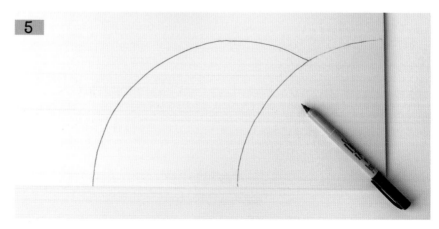

MARKING QUILT DESIGNS

My favourite way to mark my quilts is with a Hera marker. This is a small plastic tool of Japanese origin, which you use to indent your quilting designs onto the fabric. Bodkins embedded in a cork for ease of holding, or even your fingernail can do the same job, leaving a crease in the fabric that you can follow with your quilting stitch. This method is non-invasive and uses no inks, so there is no worry about harmful chemicals or needing to get rid of the marks afterwards. When the quilt is washed, any creases that weren't quilted over will disappear.

Alternative methods include a chalk wheel or Chaco Liner, a sliver of dried soap or soapstone pencils. With any method you use, do make sure that it will erase after it has served its purpose, and does not leave damaging chemical residue on your work.

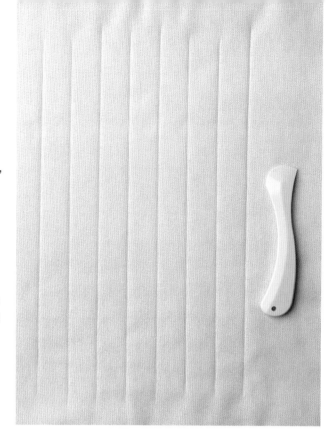

Marking a quilt

1 Place the template in the bottom RH corner of the quilt (LH corner if you are left-handed). Draw round the arc.

2 Move the template along and continue to mark the arcs. When you get to the end of a row, the design will run off the edge off the quilt. Either turn the corner, or start to mark the next row above the first.

3 The marked arc will be quilted following the curve, top to bottom, and then the inner curves quilted by eye or with a dashed line. The distance of these curves from each other is gauged by either the length of the needle you are using or by the width of the thumb knuckle. Depending on the accuracy of the quilter, the large arcs can contain varying numbers of smaller arcs.

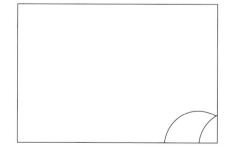 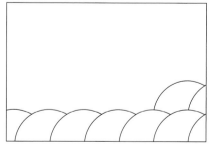 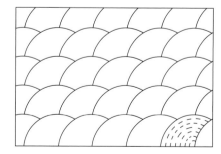

Elbow quilting

This differs from the general fan design in that the first large arc is marked by using your elbow as the pivot point for the arc, so you do not need a template. You can usually tell if a design is elbow-quilted due to the size of the first arc – these are generally larger than if you had made a template. The inner lines are gauged in the same way as the fans, and are quilted from the large curve down towards the smallest curve as before.

Thumb/egg-cup quilting

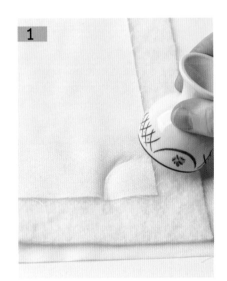

This variation of fan quilting is worked from the smallest curve outwards to the biggest curve. The numbers of curves are then counted as the fans get bigger, so all of the fans will have the same number of curves but the fans may be of slightly different sizes depending on the accuracy of the quilter.

1 Start by using your thumb to mark the size of the first curve or mark around a small household object, such as an egg cup.

2 Quilt this first marked line. You will use a needle or your thumb to measure out the spacing around the curve – mark a second line.

3 Quilt this second line and measure and mark your third quilting line as before. Stop quilting when you feel the largest curve has created a fan of the desired size, then start on the next one, remembering to quilt the same number of curves as for the first fan.

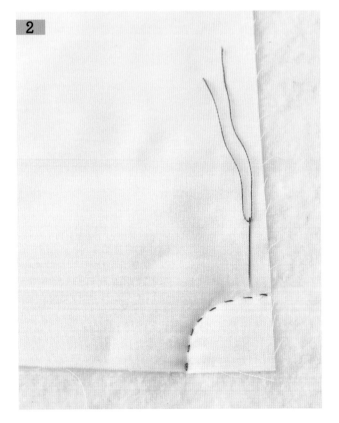

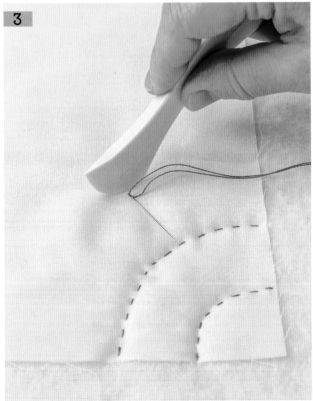

QUILTING stitches

Before you start stitching, make sure you know how to securely start and stop.
You don't want to waste time going back over stitches that have come undone.

STARTING THE STITCH

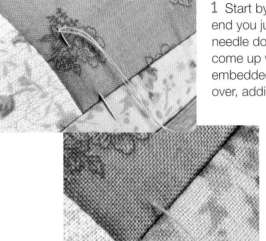

1 Start by cutting a length of thread as long as your arm. Tie a knot in the end you just cut. Thread the free end into the needle. You need to insert the needle down through the top layer of fabric and wadding/batting only to come up where you want to start, pulling on the thread so that the knot is embedded in the wadding/batting and the embedded thread will be quilted over, adding an extra layer of security for the thread.

2 If the knot won't pull through the fabric, use the point of the needle to poke the weave of the fabric to expand the hole where the knot needs to go through. Gently pull the thread until the knot goes into the wadding/batting and then, using the needle, push the threads back in place. Now you are ready to stitch.

STOPPING THE STITCH

At the end of the stitching, or if the thread is running out, you will need to finish off securely. Make sure you leave enough thread to enable you to do this – about 5–6in (15cm). It may seem a lot, but if you leave less than this, the process will be really fiddly.

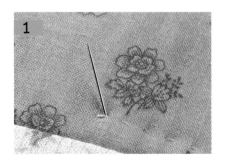

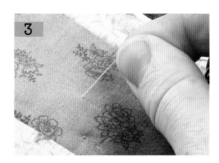

1 Make the last stitch, going all the way through to the back of the quilt with the needle, then bring the needle back up at the beginning of the last stitch.

2 Pull the thread through and wrap it around the needle two or three times (it will depend on how thick your thread is and how densely woven the fabric is; you are making a knot that will pull through easily).

3 Put the needle into the middle of the last stitch, just underneath it, going through the front fabric and wadding/batting travelling a needle's length away from the stitching. As you pull the thread, a knot will form that needs to be gently pulled through to embed in the wadding/batting. If the knot has a loop, smooth it out with your fingers before pulling it through. Snip the thread tail close to the quilt top.

BIG STITCH TIPS

This style of quilting uses a relatively thick thread and big stitches. The stitch length is often longer on the top surface of the quilt and smaller on the bottom. Big stitch quilting is a bold style of quilting and the designs are usually fairly widely spaced, therefore needing fewer lines, and taking less time to quilt.

- Follow the sequence on starting the stitch (see page 33), and continue on. As you make the stitches, try to work with a rhythm to create even but large stitches that go through all three layers.

- I keep the needle hand still with the needle horizontal and move the finger that is on the underside of the quilt to create the stitches. Try different motions to see which is comfortable for you and creates the even stitches you want.

- I find it helpful to have a thimble on the middle finger of the needle hand for pushing the needle through, and a ridged thimble on the index finger of the hand under the quilt. The finger under the quilt pushes the layers up, creating a little 'hill' with the ridge of the thimble, which the needle is pushed against to make the stitch.

- When you have about 6in (15cm) of thread left in the needle, finish off and then start a new length of thread (see page 33).

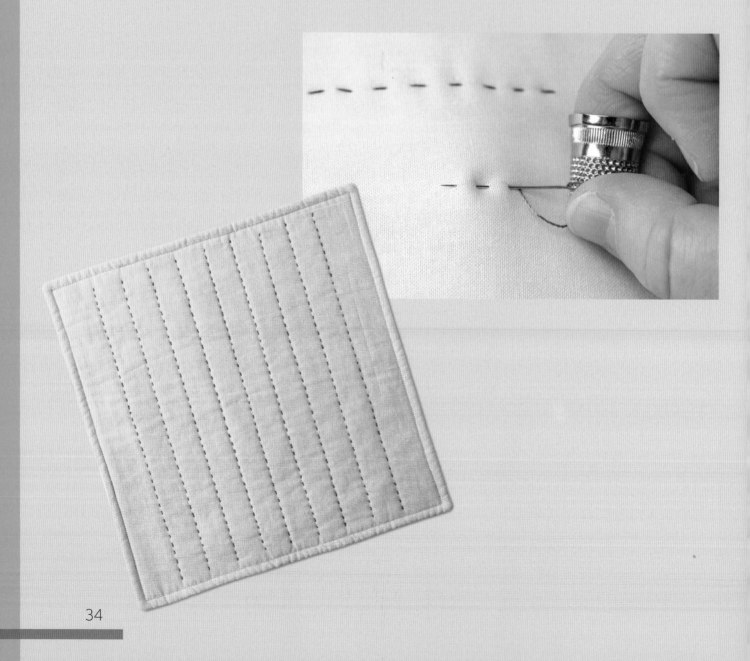

MENNONITE TACKS

This stitch holds the three layers together just like regular big stitch, but with some added texture, for a bolder look. It is a cross between a stitch and knot as the little stitch acts to secure the long stitch, stopping any puckering. The stitches can be placed in conjunction with the piecing on the quilt, i.e. at seam junctions or the centre of patches, or it can be used randomly.

How to

1 Start off by embedding the knot in the wadding/batting along the line that you will be stitching along (see page 33). Don't come up right at the start of the line, as the first part of the stitch is to go backwards, and you need to allow room to do this. Insert the needle to make a backstitch going through all the layers and coming up just before the start of the stitch and just above it.

2 Push the needle into the first two layers just below the long stitch and let the needle travel through the wadding/batting to come up at the next stitch, about a needle's length away.

3 Continue on in this way and finish off the final stitch with the little stitch that crosses the long one. The spacing of the stitches can be dependent on the length of your needle, and should form a natural rhythm.

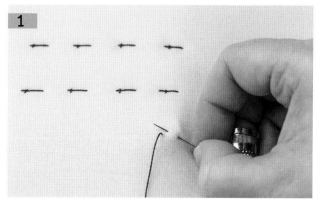

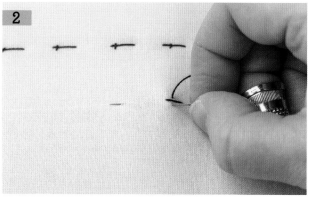

METHODIST KNOTS

This is another stitch with texture that securely holds the three layers of the quilt together. These stitches work up quickly and you can achieve a nice rhythm.

How to

1 Start off by embedding the knot in the wadding/batting along the line that you will be stitching over (see page 33). Come up through the top fabric and insert the needle down through all three layers, as if for backstitch. Do not make this stitch too big, as the stitch on the back of the quilt will be bigger, as it needs to come up ahead of this stitch. Bring the needle up about a third of the length of the backstitch in front of it.

2 Push the needle down, creating a small backstitch that meets the long first stitch, but this time only going into the wadding/batting. The needle travels along to the next stitch – to the left-hand side of the long stitch.

3 Pull the thread through to complete the first Methodist knot stitch.

4 Continue on in the same way. Finish with the small backstitch.

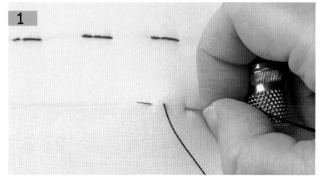

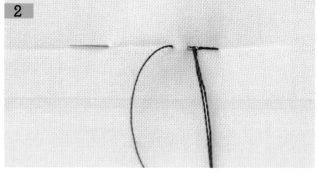

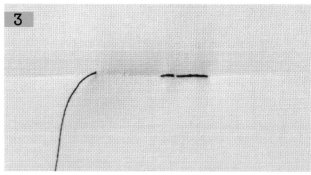

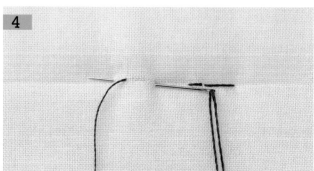

RUNNING CROSS STITCH

This stitch is a little like the Japanese sashiko stitch called 'Ten' (*juujizashi*), where rows of running stitches intersect to make little crosses. These stitches are worked one at a time in rows across the work. This stitch works well at seam junctions, rather like tying a quilt, as well as along seam lines, or in the centre of patches.

How to

1 Start off by embedding the knot in the wadding/batting along the line that you will be stitching over (see page 33). Bring the needle up through the quilt top and make a diagonal stitch going down through all of the layers to the back of the quilt, and coming back up at the top of the cross.

2 Pull the needle through.

3 Take the needle down into the top and the wadding/batting at the bottom-left of the cross. The needle needs to complete the cross stitch and then travel to the start of the next stitch.

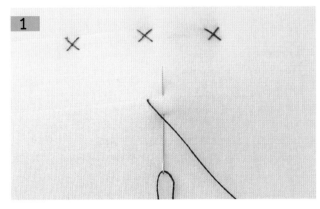

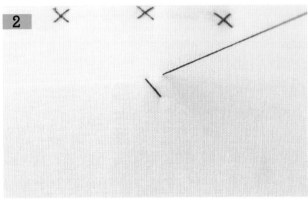

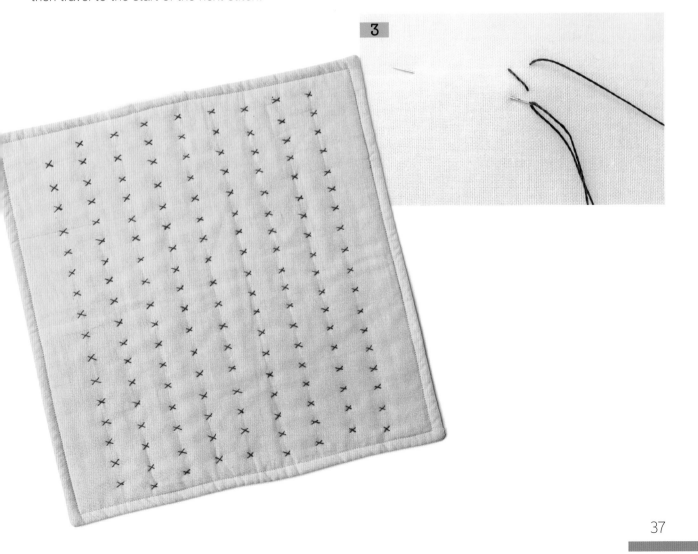

BINDING

Once the quilt is quilted, remove any tacking/basting stitches or pins. It is now ready for binding. First, I will show you how to bind your quilt with mitred corners. You need to start by joining fabric strips together to make a continuous length that goes all the way around your quilt. Use a strip width of 2½in (6.5cm).

JOINING STRIPS TOGETHER

I use a bias join for joining strips together, which results in less bulk when the fabric is folded over and wrapped around the edge of the quilt.

1 Take a fabric strip and lay a second fabric strip at 90 degrees on top of it, right sides facing. Allow an extra ⅜in (1cm) of fabric along each short edge. Stitch across the diagonal.

2 Join subsequent strips using chain piecing (see page 19). Open out the first two strips and lay a third strip face down on the end of the second strip, as in step 1. Stitch across the diagonal. Continue to add fabric strips until you have a piece that is long enough to go all round the quilt.

3 Cut through the joining threads and trim off the excess fabric at each join, leaving a ¼in (5mm) seam allowance. Press all the seams open neatly.

MOCK BIAS JOIN

Follow these steps to prepare the end of your binding for continuous mitred binding.

1 Fold in the end of the strip at 90 degrees, then fold and press the whole strip in half, WS together.

2 Trim off the excess fabric at the end of the strip, leaving a ¼in (5mm) seam allowance.

CONTINUOUS MITRED BINDING

This type of binding has a mock bias join to complete the two ends. Start by fitting an even-feed (walking) foot to your sewing machine and prepare the binding end as explained for a mock bias join, opposite.

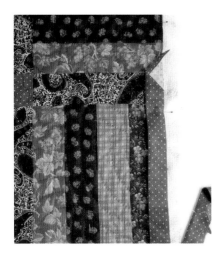

1 Lay the binding along one side of the quilt, raw edges aligned and starting about one-third of the way along. Pin it in place. I do not usually trim the wadding/batting and backing to match the quilt front until the first steps of the binding are complete, but if you want to trim them now, you can do so.

2 Using the width of the even-feed (walking) foot to gauge the binding width, start stitching about 4in (10cm) away from the end of the binding. Sew down towards the corner, stopping about ½in (1cm) away from the edge. Secure the stitches.

3 Remove the quilt from under the machine and fold the binding at 90 degrees away from the quilt so that it lies in a straight line, aligned with the next raw edge.

4 Fold the binding back down onto the quilt, aligning the raw edges and creating a fold at the corner.

5 Start sewing at the folded edge and secure the stitches. Sew down to the next corner and repeat. Turn all the corners in the same way.

6 When you get to the last side, stitch towards the join and stop about 6in (15cm) away from it. Trim the binding at an angle so that it overlaps the start by about ½in (1cm).

7 Tuck the end into the start of the binding, as shown.

8 Continue stitching along the binding to secure the two ends.

9 Remove the quilt from the sewing machine. Trim away the wadding/batting and backing fabric, if you haven't already.

10 Turn the binding over to the back of the quilt and pin it in place so that the folded edge meets up with the machine-stitched line.

11 When all the sides are pinned, fold each corner so that the bulk of the fabric lies under the fold and pin it in place.

12 Using slipstitch and a thread to match the binding, sew the binding to the backing fabric. Do not sew through to the front of the quilt, and hide the travelling stitches in the wadding/batting. When you reach the join, stitch along it.

13 Stitch the join round to the front of the fabric, then take the needle through to the back of the quilt and continue along.

14 As you reach each of the mitred corners, stitch them closed.

SQUARE-CORNERED BINDING

This is a simple basic binding to use when you want to add some colour and strength to the edge of your quilt. This version is sewn on the machine and finished by hand. Begin by cutting strips of binding 2½in (6.5cm) wide and join them with a crossway join so that you have four strips about 2in (5cm) longer than each side of the quilt. Press them in half lengthways, wrong sides together.

1 Sew one strip to the side of the quilt, matching the raw edges and using the width of the presser foot as your seam allowance. When you reach the end, trim the binding to line up with the top fabric, if necessary. Repeat this process on the opposite side of the quilt.

2 Trim off the surplus backing and wadding/batting in line with the raw edge of the binding. Finger press the binding away from the quilt top.

3 Repeat on the remaining sides of the quilt, aligning the raw edges of each strip with the raw edges of the binding strips already attached.

4 At the corners, trim away the surplus fabric and wadding/batting to make turning the binding in easier.

5 Fold the binding over onto the back of the quilt and pin it in place. Fold the corners so that the raw edges are concealed. Slipstitch the folded edge down, sewing along the open edges at the corners.

TURN THROUGH, BAGGED OUT
OR PATCH-POCKET BINDING

With this method, the quilt is, in effect, bound before it is quilted. It gives a knife-edge finish and has been popular on the kantha quilts of India and the bulkier quilts of Sweden. It is a similar process to that of turning a patch pocket or, say, the Coasters on page 98, but with the addition of wadding/batting.

Here, I have made a coaster to demonstrate the technique, which is made up of three layers of fabric: the top, backing and an interlining. In the example here, the backing and the wadding/batting are the same size as the top fabric. The coaster is not too large, and there is very little room for movement of the fabric layers when pinned together. If you are making a quilt, you will want to allow a margin of a few inches on all sides. I add 5in (13cm) to the overall measurement of the quilt to make the backing and wadding/batting larger. Once the layers are stitched together, as shown here, the backing can be trimmed to the same size as the front of the quilt, and the wadding/batting trimmed closer to the stitching line to reduce the bulk.

1 Smooth out the wadding/batting or interlining on a flat surface and temporarily secure with tape, if needed. Place the quilt backing on top of the wadding/batting, RS up, and pat flat. If you like, you can use 505 spray adhesive or safety pins here, but usually the cotton quilt back will adhere to the wadding/batting of its own accord. Place the quilt top centred, RS down on top. Pin the three layers all the way round the edge of the quilt top, with the pins perpendicular to the edge. Leave a gap in the middle of one side of about 6in (15cm) in order to turn the quilt RS out.

2 Stitch around the edge of the quilt top using a ¼in (5mm) SA, removing pins as you reach them. As you come to each corner, stitch two or three stitches across it – this will help you get a neater corner when you turn the quilt through. Secure the stitches where you start and stop, remembering to leave your 6in (15cm) turning gap.

3 Snip across the corners through all three layers. Using a pair of small sharp scissors, trim the wadding/batting close to the sewing line. Depending on the bulk of the wadding/batting, you may not need to do this.

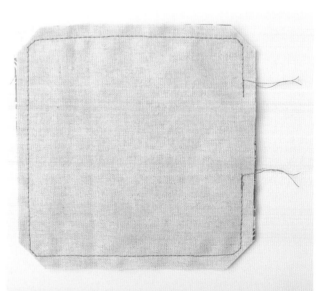

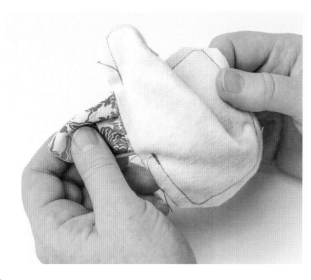

4 Turn the quilt RS out through the turning gap; pull the corner furthest from the gap through first to allow for a smooth turn through.

5 Use a pair of scissors, a chopstick or a knitting needle to carefully poke out the corners.

6 'Roll' the seam between your thumbs and forefingers to help it lie flat.

7 Either pin or use hemming clips to keep the edge flat. To keep the edge in place permanently, use a big running stitch, or one of the stitches on pages 35–37. Sew along the outside edge of the quilt just along where the bulk of the SA ends. You can now secure the three layers together if you need to, using safety pins or hand tacking/basting.

THE QUILTS

Here is a selection of nine quilts for you to make, all of them beginner friendly and all with clear step-by-step instructions and full-size templates when required. Navy Borders (page 46), Swedish Bars (page 58) and Stepping Stones (page 70) can be speeded up by using Jelly Rolls™, while you can use a Layer Cake™ for Octagons (page 52) – if you've already made an impulse buy in the quilt shop, now is the time to start using your stash! On the other hand, if you don't have any fabrics yet and want to start small, try the Quilted Vines Mini Quilt (page 88), the Dolly Quilt (page 92) or take a look at the Gifts section starting on page 96 for some other small projects that are perfect for building your confidence.

NAVY Borders

Using a plain white fabric as the framed centre of each block really highlights the quilting and lets it take centre stage. Try substituting your favourite plain as the block centre, or use shot cotton to add subtle interest. Using a wide selection of prints, including different scales and textures, adds interest to the limited colour palette of predominantly navy and white. If you haven't got too many scraps, start off with a pre-cut Jelly Roll™.

I've used big stitch quilting across the centre of the blocks, but you could use Mennonite tacks, Methodist knots or running cross stitch in the same way (see pages 35–37).

MEASUREMENTS

Quilt size: 60½in (154cm) square

Block size: 12in (30.5cm) square

REQUIREMENTS

White centres: 60in (152cm) by the width of the fabric (WoF)

Navy borders: 30 strips, 2½in (6.5cm) by WoF – as a guide for using scraps, one WoF strip will yield four (8½in/22cm) or six (6½in/16.5cm) strips

Backing: 140in (356cm) by WoF

Wadding/batting: 70 x 70in (178 x 178cm) square

Binding: 18in (50cm) by WoF

Notions: 12 wt/no. 12 blue variegated perle cotton thread

Hera marker or masking tape

FABRIC CUTTING

White centres: cut seven strips, 8½in (22cm) by WoF; sub-cut into 25 8½in (22cm) squares

Navy borders: cut 50 strips, 2½ x 8½in (6.5 x 22cm) and cut 100 strips, 2½ x 6½in (6.5 x 16.5cm)

Backing: cut into two pieces of equal length, remove the selvedge/selvage, then stitch together along the selvedge/selvage edge; press the seam open

Binding: cut seven strips, 2½in (6.5cm) by WoF. Join to a continuous length with mock bias joins (see page 38), and press the seams open. Fold in half lengthways, WS together, then press.

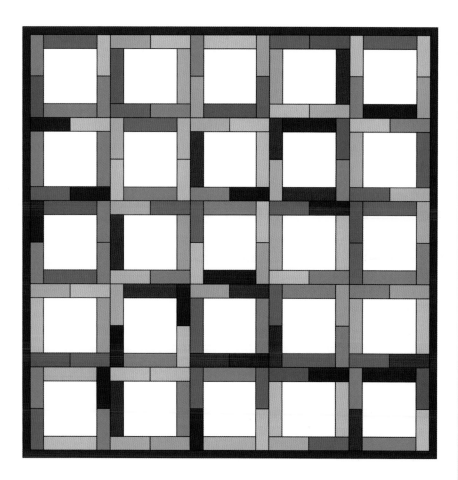

METHOD

1 Stitch two 8½in (22cm) navy border strips to opposite sides of a white centre square. Press the seams towards the strips.

2 Join a pair of 6½in (16.5cm) navy border strips together, short end to short end. Press the seam open. Repeat for a second pair.

3 Stitch the pieces made in step 2 to the remaining two opposite sides of the white block (see below). Press the seams towards the strips.

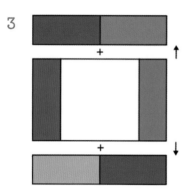

4 Repeat steps 1–3 to make 25 blocks. Arrange the blocks into five rows of five blocks. Alternate the blocks in the first row so that the side with a seam in the centre is next to a side with no central seam. In the second row, the first block will be alternating with the first block in the first row. Continue in this way until you are happy with the layout, with the block sides alternating over the whole quilt.

5 Stitch the first row together, pressing the seams towards the block with the centre seam in it. Continue to stitch the row together, pressing in this way. Stitch the remaining four rows, pressing in the same way.

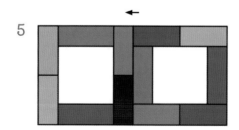

6 Stitch the rows together. Because of the way you have pressed, the seam junctions of the blocks will knit together precisely. Pin at these points if need be, and remove the pins as you stitch. Press these rows in alternating directions.

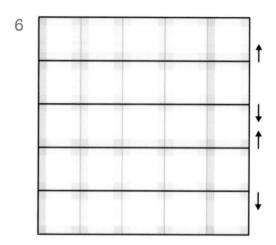

7 Layer and tack/baste the quilt top with the wadding/batting and the backing fabric.

8 I quilted this quilt using big stitches. I started by quilting in the ditch of all 25 blocks across the entire quilt (along the seam lines).

9 Each block is then quilted with lines 1in (2.5cm) apart, parallel to the 8in (20.5cm) strip block sides. You will be quilting in the ditch along two sides of the white centre. Mark the lines across the block with a ruler and Hera marker, or use masking tape as a guide. As you quilt the blocks, you will see that the lines alternate in direction, forming a basketweave effect.

10 When the quilting is finished, remove any tacking/basting, then bind and label your quilt (see below).

Labelling your quilts

Once your quilt is sewn and bound, it is worth giving a thought to labelling it. Quilts are designed to last a very long time, and a label bearing your name and the date will serve as an enduring reminder of your quilt's origins. If it is for a gift, you can add a short message and perhaps the recipient's name too. You could write directly onto the back of the quilt, write onto a label and stitch it on, embroider a message or buy a pre-printed label to attach.

I used variegated perle cotton for big stitching this quilt, to add subtle variation, but you can, of course, use plain thread. By the time you've finished working this quilt, your stitches will be neat and even. But don't worry too much about being precise. The slight variations are all part of the handmade look.

OCTAGONS

This is a great quilt for showcasing your favourite collection of fabrics from a pre-cut Layer Cake™, or for using up bold, larger prints, which would be lost if cut too small. Make sure the background and border fabric have a good contrast to the prints you use for the octagons to give maximum impact. If you like, choose a different fabric for the border to give this quilt a whole new look.

The octagon block is quick and easy to stitch, and omits the need for setting in fiddly seams: we'll use a stitch-and-flip method on the corners for minimum fuss.

The wave quilting in a neutral colour is a classic design that gives unity to the quilt and never loses its charm. It is quick and comfortable to quilt.

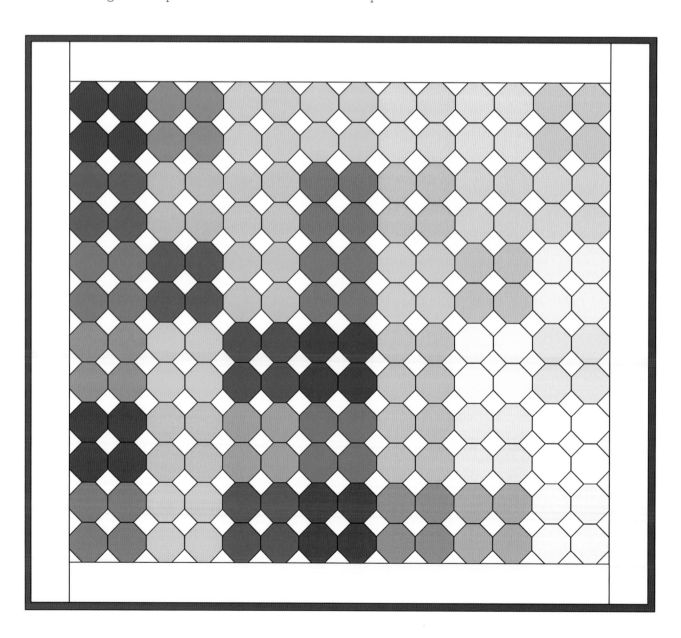

MEASUREMENTS

Quilt size: 66½ x 75½in (169 x 192cm)

Block size: 9in (23cm) square

REQUIREMENTS

Blocks: 42 10in (25.5cm) squares OR one Layer Cake™ OR four Charm Square™ packs

Background: 55in (140cm) by WoF

Border: 46in (120cm) by WoF

The background and border fabrics can be the same, as shown, or different

Wadding/batting: 76 x 85in (193 x 216cm)

Binding: 20in (55cm) by WoF

Backing: 152in (386cm) by WoF

Notions: template for wave quilting design (see page 140)

1 x 6in (2.5 x 15.25cm) rotary cutting ruler

Valdani variegated cotton perle no. 12

Propelling/mechanical marking pencil to show up on the back of the background fabric

FABRIC CUTTING

Blocks: cut each of the 42 10in (25.5cm) squares into four 5in (13cm) squares (you won't need to do this if you're using the Charm Squares™)

Background: cut 31 strips, 1¾in (4.5cm) by WoF, then sub-cut 672 1¾in (4.5cm) squares

Border: cut seven strips, 6½in (16.5cm) by WoF. Remove the selvedge/selvage and join the short ends RS together to make a continuous length. Press the seams open. Cut two border pieces 63½ x 6½in (161.5 x 16.5cm) and cut two border pieces 66½ x 6½in (169 x 16.5cm)

Binding: cut eight strips, 2½in (6.5cm) by WoF. Join to a continuous length with mock bias joins (see page 38). Press the seams open. Fold the length of the binding WS together, then press

Backing: cut the fabric into two equal lengths, remove the selvedge/selvage and stitch together along the length, pressing the seam open.

METHOD

1 For one block, take 16 1¾in (4.5cm) background squares, and draw a diagonal line on the back of each with a fine pencil.

2 Place four of these RS together on the front of one of the 5in (13cm) squares, placing them in each corner with the diagonal lines running from straight side to straight side (as shown right).

3 Stitch along the diagonal lines. If you know you'll end up stitching to one side of the line, err towards the outer corner side of the line. This will mean that when you 'stitch and flip', your new square won't be too small.

4 Now trim off the excess of both fabrics at the corners, leaving a ¼in (5mm) SA.

5 Press the seam allowances of two opposite corners towards the square, and the remaining two away from the square (as shown right). You could press these seams open, but there will be more pinning at the next stage, and I prefer to press so that the seams will nest. It means you won't have to pin so much, which makes the stitching quicker.

6 Make three more octagons in the same way.

2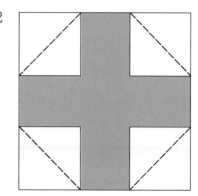

5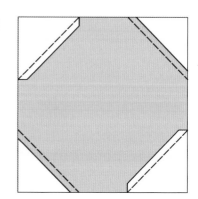

7 To join the four octagons together into a four-patch block, first place two patches RS together so that the seams knit together – they will be going in the opposite directions. Pin if this helps. Stitch the patches together into two sets of two. Press the seam open. Now join the two units RS together. Pin in the centre where the open seams come together. The remaining seams should knit together as before. Stitch and press open. Make 42 blocks in the same way.

8 Arrange the 42 blocks into seven rows of six blocks. In this version, I've tried to grade the fabrics from light to dark, but use whatever layout pleases you. It helps with this sort of layout to look through a sheet of red plastic (or similar) as you view the layout. This will give you a tonal value of the fabrics, and make the colours less distracting. Alternatively, take photographs as you work and edit them to monochrome when you view them. When you are happy with your layout, make sure the blocks in each row will have interlinking seams as before within each block. By doing this, each row will also have interlinking seams too.

9 Stitch each row together, pressing the seams open. Now sew the rows together. Pin as needed and press the seams open.

10 Stitch the borders onto the longest opposite sides first (use the 63½ x 6½in pieces). Press the seams towards the border. Now stitch the remaining two border pieces onto the remaining sides. Press as before.

11 Layer and tack/baste the quilt to the backing and wadding/batting, ready for quilting.

12 Use the template on page 140 to mark the quilting design. If you are right-handed, start in the bottom-right corner, and if you are left-handed start in the bottom-left corner. Mark and quilt the waves along the bottom side of the quilt. When this is complete, start on the row above. The design continues in this way, working up from the bottom, until the quilting is complete.

13 Remove the tacking/basting, then bind and label your quilt (see box on page 48).

7
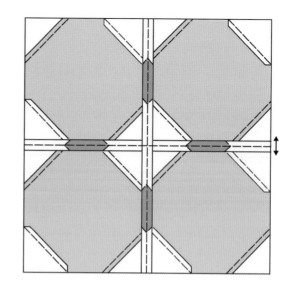

SWEDISH bars

This bold, cosy quilt was inspired by the vintage quilts of Sweden. Simple shapes, heavy fabrics and wool wadding/batting are characteristic of their quilts, all lending themselves to bold quilting and big stitches using heavier thread.

I've used quilting cotton for the bars, but a cotton-linen mix for the wide border. The quilt is unbound, with a knife-edge style finish, another Swedish characteristic, which in this case is made using the bagging out method (see pages 42–43). The border is simply quilted with more designs common to the old Swedish style of quilt making: I used straight lines and a simple flower motif.

One of the great charms of this design is that each person who makes it can truly make it their own, not just through fabric choice, but also in how they choose to lay out the units of rectangles.

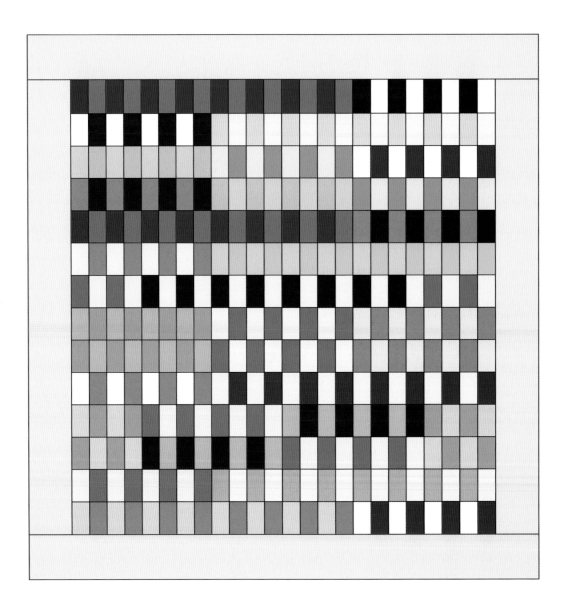

MEASUREMENTS

Quilt size: 64 x 79in
(163 x 201cm)

REQUIREMENTS

Bars: one Jelly Roll™
OR 42 strips, 2½in (6.5cm)
by WoF
OR one Layer Cake™
OR 42 squares, 10 x 10in
(25.5 x 25.5cm)

Border: Essex linen (cotton-
linen mix), 60in (153cm) by
WoF

Wadding/batting: 80 per
cent cotton/20 per cent
polyester, 69 x 84in
(175.5 x 213.5cm)

Backing: 148in (376cm)
by WoF

Notions: quilting templates A
and B (see page 140)

Valdani variegated cotton
perle no. 12

FABRIC CUTTING

Border: cut seven strips, 8½in
(21.5cm) by WoF.
Trim the selvedge/selvage
and join to a continuous
length along the short ends.
Press the seams open. Cut
two pieces, 8½ x 63½in
(21.5 x 161.5cm) and cut two
pieces, 8½ x 64½in
(21.5 x 164cm)

Backing: cut the fabric into
two equal lengths, remove the
selvedge/selvage, and join,
pressing the seam open.

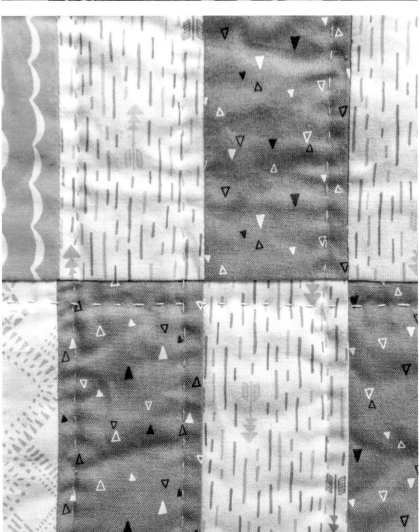

METHOD

1 Whether you use Layer Cakes™ (or 10in/25.5cm squares) or Jelly Rolls™ (or 2½in/6.5cm strips), pair up all of the fabrics – there will be 21 sets in total. I try to have combinations of contrasting designs, tones or colours to make the groupings interesting.

2 To stitch the 10in (25.5cm) squares, place a pair RS together. Stitch along opposite sides (see illustration, right).

3 Cut in half down the centre, parallel to the stitched sides. Stitch along the newly cut sides (see illustration, right).

4 Cut each in half down the centre, parallel to the stitched sides. Cut these into two 5in (12.75cm) sections (see illustration, right). Press the seams open.

5 To stitch the units using Jelly Rolls™, stitch the paired strips along their length. Press the seam open. Sub-cut into eight 5in (12.75cm) sections.

6 You will now have eight units. These will be the building blocks for your rows in the quilt. Each row will need 12 units; you will make 14 rows (so 168 units in total). You may choose to stitch these all together to make part of one long row, and group others in sections of four or two. Have fun with the placement, creating bold areas of all of the units together, and others where they are split across two rows. Use the placement in my quilt as a guide, but play until you are happy with your layout.

7 Once the centre of the quilt top is arranged, sew each row of 12 units together, pressing the seams in one direction. Then sew the rows together, again, pressing the seams in one direction.

8 Stitch the 63½in (161.5cm) borders to opposite sides of the quilt top. Press the seams towards the border. Stitch the remaining two borders to the top and bottom of the quilt; press the seams to the borders.

9 Lay out the wadding/batting, then the backing RS up. Place the quilt top RS down, and centred. Follow steps 1–6 on pages 42–43 for bagging out the quilt.

2

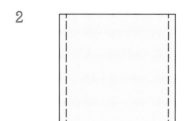

3

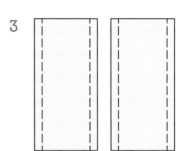

4

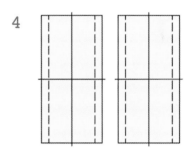

6

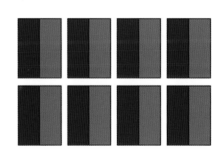

10 Once the quilt is RS out and you have rolled the edges flat, tack/baste them in place. Pat the layers flat so as to avoid unnecessary stretching. Tack/baste the layers of the rest of the quilt together (see page 25).

11 Quilt around the edge of the quilt, using the SA as a guide to quilt ¼in (5mm) from the edge, removing the tacking/basting as you go.

12 Quilt the patchworked centre of the quilt by quilting ¼in (5mm) from the seams on one side of the rows and then one side of the columns.

13 Quilt the border all the way around the patchworked centre ¼in (5mm) from the seam – again the SA can act as a guide.

14 Use the rotary cutting ruler to mark the corner quilting. Line up the 45-degree angle with the straight side of the quilt and draw a line from one side to the other across and just touching the tip of the patchwork corner. Mark a further six lines spaced 1½in (4cm) apart. Quilt. (Refer to the image on page 59.)

15 On the short sides of the quilt, mark a centre triangle using your ruler (mine measures 7in/18cm tall, and 14in/35.5cm wide). Fill this in with two inner triangles 1½in (4cm) apart (shown opposite, top).

16 On the long sides, mark the border with another triangle in the middle and another two on either side at the quarter points, filling in with inner triangles as before. Use templates A and B on page 140, the flower and flower centre, to quilt between the triangles to finish (shown opposite, bottom).

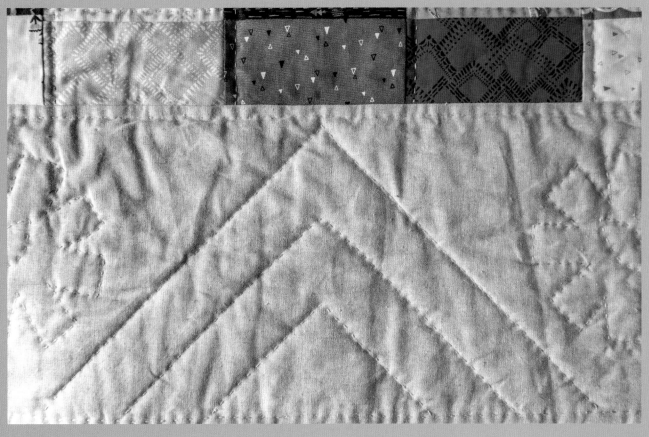

FABRIC stack

This quilt celebrates the sheer joy of fabric: to me it is reminiscent of piles of fabric sitting on top of each other waiting to become a quilt. It was inspired by a quilt from a book by Roderick Kiracofe, *Unconventional and Unexpected*.

This is a celebration of one of my favourite colours: blue. You can use your favourite colour, or even style of print, designer or fabric collection. The pieces are large, so big prints work well, but I have combined these with mid-scale prints as well as checks, toile and Ikat weave. All of these elements keep your eye roving around the quilt.

Although I have to provide fabric requirements for the purposes of this book, I would suggest you use as many or as few fabrics as you like. I would recommend a minimum of 24, but it's your quilt, your stash and it's up to you.

In the same way, the quilting will be individual to you. The wave design uses the elbow span from hand to elbow (see page 32), so everyone's will be slightly different depending on how you hold the marker and how long your arms are. The big stitch quilting adds to the boldness, the fun and the speed of making this quilt.

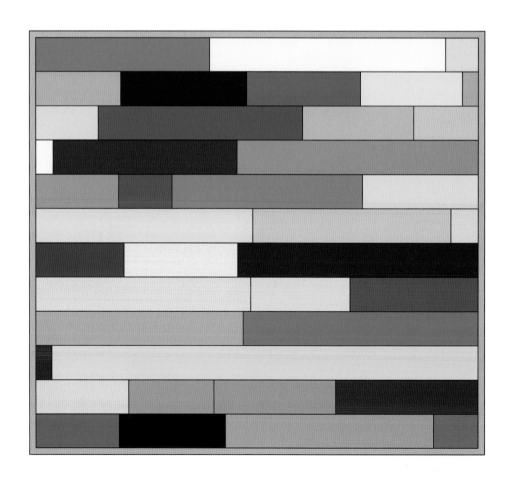

MEASUREMENTS

Quilt size: 80½ x 72½in (205 x 184cm)

REQUIREMENTS

Fabric strips: use a minimum of 24 different fabrics, with all strips 6½in (16.5cm) wide

Row 1: 30½in (77.5cm); 43½in (110.5cm); 7½in (19cm)

Row 2: 15½in (39.5cm); 20½in (52cm); 21½in (54.5cm); 21½in (54.5cm); 3½in (9cm)

Row 3: 10½in (27cm); 39½in (100.5cm); 20½in (52cm); 10½in (27cm)

Row 4: 3½in (9cm); 34in (86.5cm); 44in (112cm)

Row 5: 16½in (42cm); 9in (23cm); 33½in (85cm); 22½in (57cm)

Row 6: 40½in (103cm); 34½in (88cm); 6½in (16.5cm)

Row 7: 17½in (44.5cm); 22in (56cm); 42in (107cm)

Row 8: 41½in (105.5cm); 17in (43cm); 23in (58.5cm)

Row 9: 40½in (103cm); 40½in (103cm)

Row 10: 3½in (9cm); 77½in (197cm)

Row 11: 19½in (49.5cm); 19½in (49.5cm); 20½in (52cm); 22½in (57cm)

Row 12: 18½in (47cm); 20½in (52cm); 33½in (85cm); 8½in (21.5cm)

Backing: 164in (420cm) by WoF

Wadding/batting: 90 x 82in (229 x 208.5cm)

Binding: 20in (55cm) by WoF

Notions: Hera marker for marking the quilt lines

Valdani variegated cotton perle no. 12

FABRIC CUTTING

Fabric strips: as above

Backing: cut the fabric into two equal lengths, remove the selvedge/selvage and stitch together along the length, pressing the seam open

Binding: cut eight strips, 2½in (6.5cm) by WoF. Join with mock bias joins (see page 38) to make one long length, pressing the seams open. Fold along the length, WS together and press.

METHOD

1 Stitch the chosen fabrics in each row together along their short ends. Press the seams in any direction – as none of the seams in the rows match up, it will not matter which direction you press. Check that each row measures 80½in (205cm) in length and trim as needed.

2 Once the 12 rows are complete, stitch them together. Start by pinning two rows RS facing, pinning the start and the end of the row, then the halfway point, followed by the quarter points. I find it easier to stitch all of the rows into pairs, press the seams (in any direction) then stitch these into two groups of three pairs. Press the seams again, then finally stitch the two halves of the quilt together; press the seam.

3 Layer the top with wadding/batting and backing fabric and tack/baste together (see page 25).

4 The quilting on this quilt is elbow quilting, which makes large Baptist fan waves (see page 32). To start, hold the Hera marker in your right hand, and place your elbow in the bottom right-hand corner of the quilt. (If you are left-handed, the elbow should go in the bottom left-hand corner.) Mark an arc from one raw edge to the other (to make a quarter-circle). Now move your arm along so the elbow is resting where the last arc was drawn. Again, using the elbow as the pivot, mark an arc from the raw edge of the quilt to the last arc marked. This will be your wave design.

5 Start quilting the large arcs, then fill in with smaller arcs. These are usually spaced to the length of your quilting needle, or the depth of the top of your thumb to the first joint (see page 32).

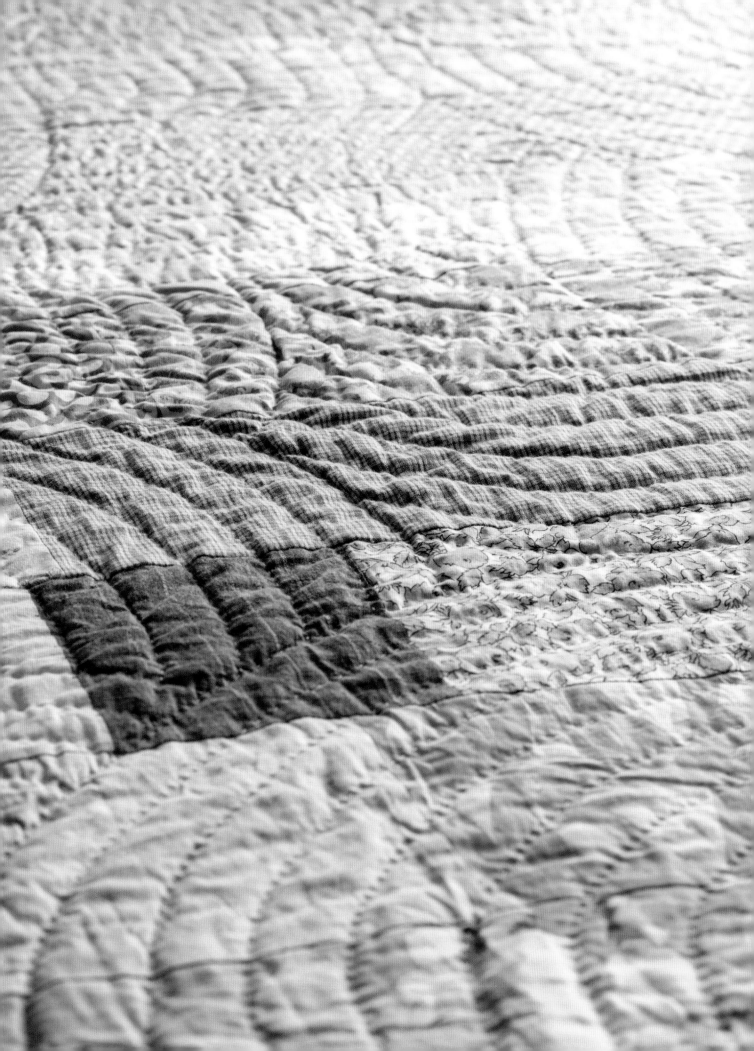

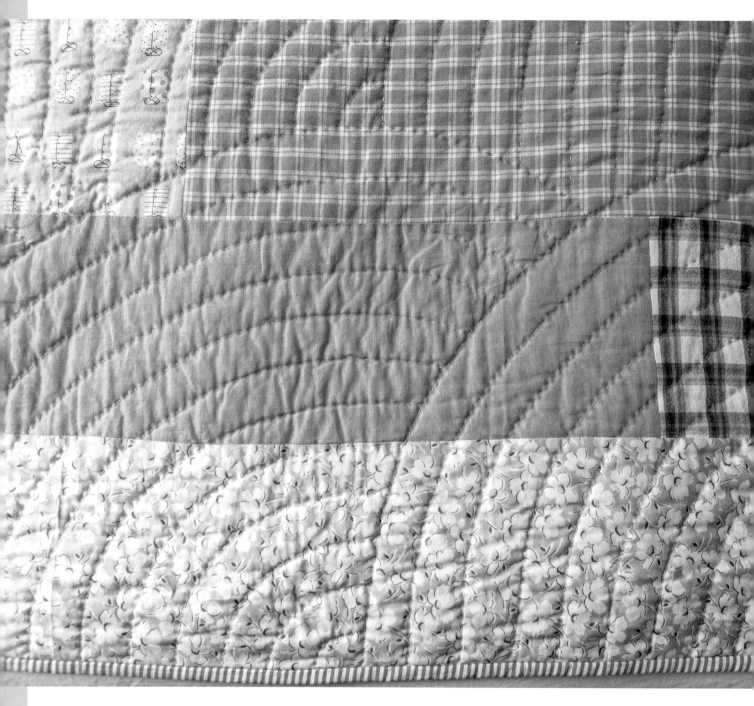

6 When one side is complete, continue all the way around the outside edge. Then move into the centre, repeating the process until the quilt is completely quilted (see also page 29).

7 Prepare the quilt for binding and labelling. This quilt uses the square-cornered binding method – follow the steps on page 41 to attach the binding. See the box on page 48 for some advice on labelling.

STEPPING stones

This quilt is inspired by a simple scrap utility quilt. The process of stitching is relatively quick, which, combined with big stitch quilting, means you can get this quilt on a bed fast! The quilting pattern is quick to work as it follows the grid of the patchwork, and requires very little, if any, marking. Use a contrasting thread if you want the pattern to be more dominant, especially across the large rectangles.

The large turquoise rectangles in this quilt are cut from shot cotton, in which the warp and weft are different colours. This means that, depending on the direction of placement in the quilt, they will look a slightly different colour, which adds to the textural interest.

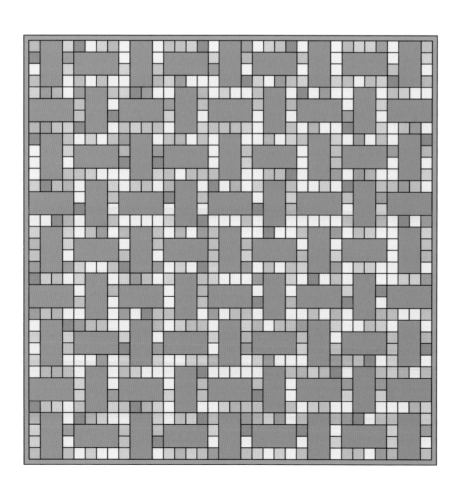

MEASUREMENTS

Quilt size: 72½in (184cm) square

Block size: 8in (20.5cm) square

REQUIREMENTS

Blue fabric: 94in (240cm) by WoF

Fabric scraps: 41 strips, 2½in (6.5cm) by WoF – a Jelly Roll™ will provide nearly all of these, and if you buy extra backing or binding you'll make up the extra

Wadding/batting: 82 x 82in (210 x 210cm)

Backing: 164in (420cm) by WoF

Binding: 20in (55cm) by WoF

Notions: Aurifil 12wt thread

FABRIC CUTTING

Blue: cut 11 strips, 8½in (21.5cm) by WoF. Sub-cut into 81 rectangles, 4½ x 8½in (11.5 x 21.5cm)

Fabric scraps: sub-cut strips into 656 squares, 2½ x 2½in (6.5 x 6.5cm); as a guide, one 2½in (6.5cm) strip by WoF will yield 16 squares

Backing: cut into two pieces of equal length, remove selvedge/selvage. Stitch together along the selvedge/selvage edge, then press the seam open

Binding: cut eight pieces, 2½in (6.5cm) by WoF. Join to make a continuous length with mock bias joins (see page 38). Press the seams open. Fold in half along the length, WS together, and press.

Tip

If you have other pre-cuts rather than Jelly Rolls™, do use them as they easily cut to the square size. As a guide, one 5in (13cm) square yields four 2½in (6.5cm) squares, so you would need 164 5in (13cm) squares. One 10in (25.5cm) square will yield 16 2½in (6.5cm) squares, so you will need 41 of them.

METHOD

1 Stitch a set of four 2½in (6.5cm) squares together into a row. Repeat to create a second row. The pressing is very important here, as it will make all of the blocks fit together easily when you get to that stage: press the seams on either end away from the centre. The middle seam can go in either direction, but the first two are important.

2 Stitch one of these rows to each long side of a blue rectangle. Press the seams towards the rectangle, as shown.

3 Repeat steps 1–2 to create 81 blocks (you will have eight 2½in/6.5cm squares left over, which can be saved for another project).

4 Arrange the blocks, alternating their direction, into nine rows of nine blocks (see the quilt illustration on page 70). Because of the pressing, the seam junctions should knit together, but pin to secure if you like (remember that you'll need to remove the pins as you stitch).

5 Stitch each row together; press the seams towards the adjoining turquoise rectangles.

6 Stitch the rows together, again pinning the seam junctions. Press the rows in alternating directions: the seam should be pressed towards the row with the most adjoining turquoise rectangles.

7 Layer and tack/baste the quilt with the wadding/batting and backing fabric (see page 25).

8 The quilting is in a simple grid design, which follows the seams of the blocks. Quilt in the ditch and then follow the grid over the rectangles. Mark this or work by eye. When the quilting is complete, remove the tacking/basting. Bind and label your quilt (see pages 38–41 for binding, and page 48 for labelling).

2
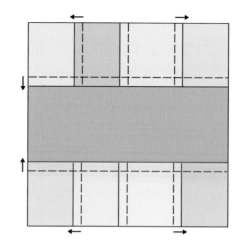

4
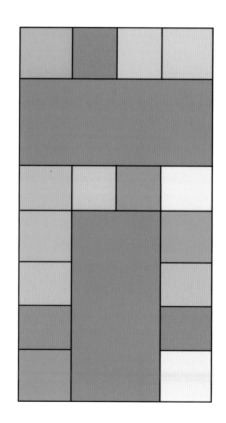

EVERY last piece

This quilt contains a lot of blocks and these can be stitched over a long time period if you like, so as not to be overwhelming. You can then speed up the making of the quilt using big stitch quilting!

The design was inspired by a vintage quilt in my collection, and the original maker had no regard for the niceties of the maths required for the half-square and quarter-square triangles in the outside edge units. In keeping with the original, I, too, have just used the basic unit with no special maths, and hence the outside edge of your quilt may need to be straightened up when you sew the border onto the pieced quilt.

Fabric choices for this quilt can play a large part in the look of it. If you choose fabrics with a large all-over print, they will give a completely different look in each square when cut to size. Equally, having some fabrics with small prints, checks and spots will give a nice contrast and repetition over the quilt.

If you would like some consistency in the blocks, pick a particular colour of print to go in the centre of each block. For this, allow 7½in (20cm) of fabric. Cut five 1½in (4cm) strips by the width of the fabric. These five strips can substitute five strips from the scrap strips given in the Requirements box on page 78. This quilt uses the sew-then-cut method (see pages 20–21); if you prefer to sew the squares individually then you will need to cut your fabric accordingly.

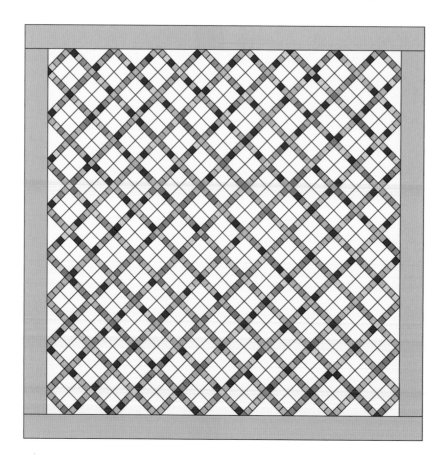

MEASUREMENTS

Quilt size: 69½in (177cm) square

Block size: 5in (13cm) square

REQUIREMENTS

White fabric: 80in (203cm) by WoF

Scraps: 45 strips, 1½in (4cm) by WoF OR 40 strips if substituting five of these for a consistent fabric, as noted in the introduction

Border: 46in (120cm) by WoF

Wadding/batting: 80 x 80in (204 x 204cm)

Backing: 160in (408cm) by WoF

Binding: 20in (55cm) by WoF

Notions: rotary cutting ruler, 16 x 5½in (41 x 14cm), for marking border quilting design

Aurifil 12wt thread

FABRIC CUTTING

White fabric: cut 32 strips, 2½in (6.5cm) by WoF. Sub-cut into 512 squares, 2½ x 2½in (6.5 x 6.5cm)

Scraps: each strip will yield 26 1½ (4cm) squares, but do not cut at this stage

Border: cut seven strips, 6½in (16.5cm) by WoF. Remove the selvedge/selvage and join the short sides to form a continuous length. Press the seams open. Sub-cut this length into two 6½ x 57½in (16.5 x 146cm) pieces and two 6½ x 69½in (16.5 x 177cm) pieces

Binding: cut eight strips, 2½in (6.5cm) by WoF. Join the short sides to form a continuous length with a mock bias join (see page 38). Press the seams open. Fold along the length, WS together, then press

Backing: cut into two equal lengths. Remove the selvedge/selvage and stitch together along these edges. Press the seam open.

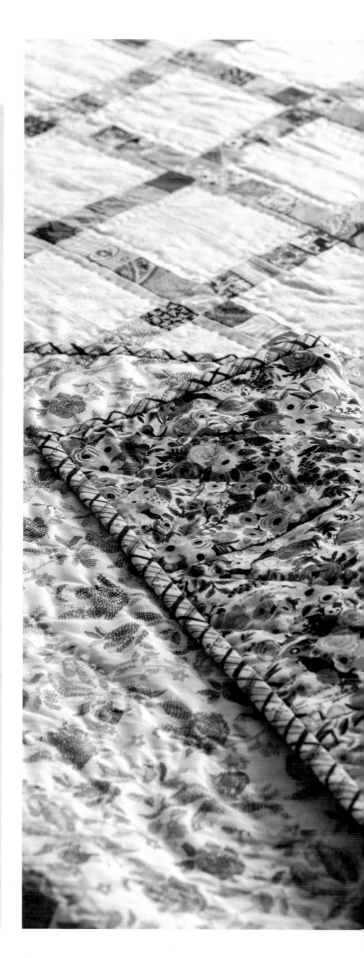

METHOD

1 Here, we are going to use the sew-then-cut method to make and join all the little squares in a manageable way. Stitch 20 1½in (4cm) strips together in pairs. Press the seams in one direction – it will not matter which direction at this stage. Sub-cut into 256 1½in (4cm) two-square units.

2 Stitch a 2½in (6.5cm) background square to either side of a two-square unit, creating a four-square unit. Press the seams towards the background squares. Make 256 of these four-square units. If you press the seams as suggested here you will create small blocks which, when put together into larger blocks, will have nesting seams. This will save you time as it means you do not need to pin all of the seams together when you come to sew them. However, if you want, press all of the seams open at every stage, but remember to pin to make sure the seams do not slip.

3 Stitch 20 strips of fabric together in pairs. Take the remaining five scrap strips or the five strips of consistent fabric, and sew a pair of strips to the side of each. Each central strip will now have a set of paired strips sewn either side. Press the seams towards the centre fabric. Sub-cut into 1½in (4cm) strips to make 128 of these five-square units.

4 Stitch a four-square unit to either side of this five-square strip. Press the seams towards the strip. Make 128 of these units.

5 Now stitch four of these units together to make a four-patch type block. You can see that if you place the four blocks correctly, the seams will nest together. Press the seams open for this block.

4

5

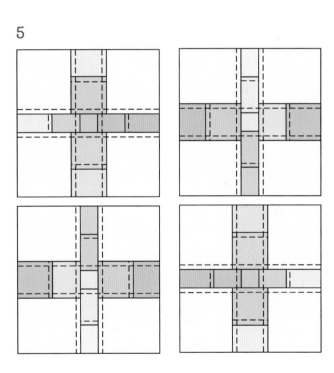

6 Lay out 25 of these units as shown in the illustration, right. Cut six units in half diagonally and position these twelve half-square blocks on the ends of the rows. Use the remaining unit and cut into quarters. Place these quarter-blocks at the corners.

7 Stitch the quilt together in diagonal rows as shown; press the seams in alternating directions on each row.

8 Now stitch the rows together, pinning as needed to keep the seams in line. Press the seams open.

9 Stitch the two short borders onto opposite sides of the quilt. Press the seams towards the border. Stitch the remaining two borders on the remaining two sides. Press the seams towards the border.

10 Layer and tack/baste with backing and wadding/batting ready to quilt (see page 25).

11 Quilt ¼in (5mm) in from the edges of the patches on the background fabric, using the SA as a guide. Stitch in long lines, skipping the needle behind the patched strips so that you do not have to keep stopping and starting. Stitch right up to the patch before skipping. Stop at the border fabric.

12 Quilt around the border ¼in (5mm) in from the seam. Now mark the border quilting, referring to the illustration, right. This is the same grid, but offset from the one on the main quilt. If you like, you could just continue with the same grid, marking it on the border.

13 When the quilting is complete, remove the tacking/basting. Bind using the continuous mitred method (see pages 39–40) and label the quilt (see box on page 48).

6

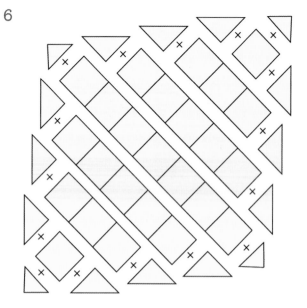

12

SCATTERED flowers

Machine quilted by The Quilt Room, Dorking, Surrey.

This quilt uses the best of both hand and machine quilting in the same project. Unusually, too, the appliqué flowers are stitched on after the machine quilting is finished. I like the raised effect that this gives the appliqué, and it also means that you do not have to navigate machine quilting around the flowers. Big stitch quilting in a contrasting thread acts as a nice contrast to the neutral machine quilting and gives a good texture too. I used the freezer-paper method for the appliqué, but you can use your favourite method.

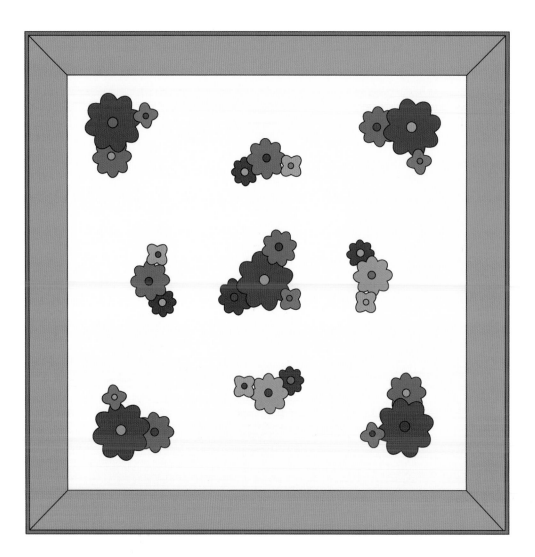

MEASUREMENTS

Quilt size: 76½in (195cm) square

REQUIREMENTS

Cream: 125in (320cm) by WoF

Border: 60in (153cm) by WoF OR 80in (205cm) by WoF if cutting strips parallel to the selvedge/selvage and no need to join

Appliqué flowers for the centre and four corners:

L, five 9in (23cm) squares

CL, five 3in (7.5cm) squares

M, six 6½in (16.5cm) squares

CM, six 2in (5cm) squares

S1, five 4½in (11.5cm) squares

CS, five 1½in (4cm) squares

Appliqué flowers for the quarter-points:

M, four 6½in (16.5cm) squares

CM, four 2in (5cm) squares

S1, four 4½in (11.5cm) squares

CS, four 1½in (4cm) squares

S2, four 4½in (11.5cm) squares

CS, four 1½in (4cm) squares

Wadding/batting: 86 x 86in (219 x 219cm)

Backing: 172in (440cm) by WoF

Binding: 20in (55cm) by WoF

Notions: flower templates – CS, CM, CL, S1, S2, M, L (see pages 142 and 143)

Freezer paper

Hera marker

Valdani variegated cotton perle no. 12

FABRIC CUTTING

Cream: cut into two equal 62½in (160cm) widths. Remove the selvedges/selvages and split one length down the middle. Attach this to either side of the other length; press the seams open. Trim to a 62½in (160cm) square

Border: cut eight strips, 7½in (19cm) by WoF. Trim selvedges/selvages and join to make a continuous length, pressing the seams open. Cut this into four 80in (203cm) lengths
OR if cutting parallel to the selvedge/selvage from 80in (203cm), cut four strips, 7½ x 80in (19 x 203cm) wide

Appliqué flowers and centres: using the templates, cut freezer-paper shapes for each flower and centre. Iron the shiny side to the WS of the fabric, and then cut out, adding a scant ¼in (5mm) SA. Using a tacking/basting thread, turn the SA over the edge of the paper and secure with tacking/basting stitches. Snip into the fabric as needed to ensure a smooth curve. Start and finish the tacking/basting on the RS of the flower so it is easier to remove the tacking/basting later

Backing: cut into two equal lengths. Remove the selvedge/selvage and join, pressing the seam open

Binding: cut eight strips, 2½in (6.5cm) by WoF. Join to a continuous length with mock bias joins (see page 38). Press the seams open. Fold in half along the length, WS together, then press.

METHOD

1 To stitch the borders with mitred corners, first find the middle of each side of the quilt top, and either press or pin to mark. Do the same with each border strip.

2 Pin a border RS together along one side of the quilt-top fabric, making sure the centre points match. You will have extra fabric extending beyond each end of the quilt top. Stitch the border in place, making sure you start and stop stitching ¼in (5mm) from the raw edge of the quilt top. Repeat this on all four sides. Press the seams towards the borders.

3 To mitre the border, work from the WS of the fabrics. Overlap the borders at the corner and use a ruler and Hera marker to mark the crease at the diagonal, from the corner of the quilt-top fabric to the point where the two borders overlap (see illustration 3a, right). Mark both fabrics, and then trim to leave each a ¼in (5mm) SA (see illustration 3b, right).

4 Pin this seam RS together along the crease, and stitch together. Remember to stop when you reach the stitches at the corner where it meets the quilt top. Press the seams open (see illustration, right). Repeat on all four corners.

5 Now layer and tack/baste the quilt for machine quilting (see page 25). Machine quilt using a 1¼in (4cm) grid across the centre and the border fabric. If you like, you can now bind the quilt (see pages 38–40).

6 The quilt is now ready to have the appliqué and big stitch quilting added. Position the flowers as shown on the illustration, page 82. The following measurements are for guidance, so do feel free to place them as you like, or even add some more: the corner flower, L, 3½in (9cm) in from the border; the quarter-point flowers, M, 10in (25.5cm) in from the border.

7 Pin the flowers in place and stitch down, without stitching through to the back of the quilt. Start and stop stitching on a straight or straight-ish side of the shape. When you return to the starting point, stop an inch or so away, remove the tacking/basting and take the paper out, before finishing the stitching. For any shapes that overlap, stitch down the underneath ones first. Stitch the centre circles down once the flowers are attached.

8 I then used big stitch quilting in a contrasting green thread to quilt all the way around the cream fabric, ¼in (5mm) from the border, and around the flower groupings (see the photo opposite, top).

9 Then, using the machine quilting as a guide, I quilted a grid surrounding the flowers, about three grid squares long. I did this for the central grouping and the corner ones (see the photo opposite, bottom for the placement of the big-stitch grid).

3a
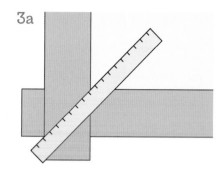

3b
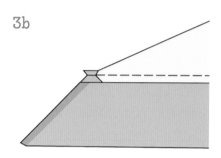

4
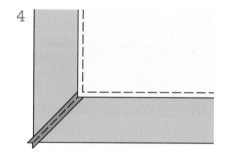

QUILTED VINES
mini quilt

This little quilt was inspired by lovely 1950s fabric designs in which shapes of colour had designs drawn over them in black. In some cases the shapes were the same, while in others the drawn design seems to bear little relation to the shapes and colours. These designs, by Lucienne Day and other textile designers of the time, inspired the use of these abstract colours and the shapes of the quilted vines and leaves.

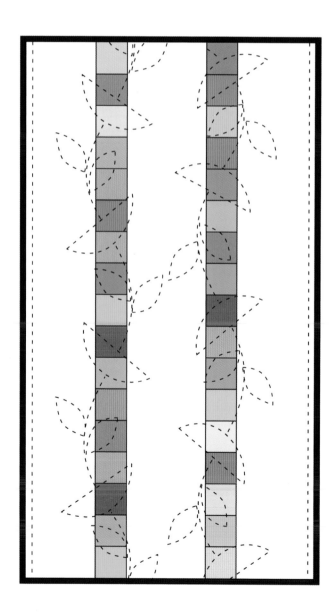

MEASUREMENTS

Quilt size: 34½ x 19½in (88 x 49.5cm)

REQUIREMENTS

Fabric scraps: 34 squares, 2½ x 2½in (6.5 x 6.5cm)

White Essex linen: 18in (46cm) by WoF

Wadding/batting: 40 x 25in (102 x 64cm)

Backing: 25in (64cm) by WoF

Binding: 8in (20.5cm) by WoF

Notions: leaf, flower and curve templates (see page 141)

Valdani black cotton perle no. 12

FABRIC CUTTING

Fabric scraps: see above

White linen: cut three strips, 5½in (14cm) by WoF. Trim the selvedge/selvage off and cut each to measure 34½in (88cm) long

Backing: 40 x 25in (102 x 63.5cm)

Binding: cut three strips, 2½in (6.5cm) by WoF. Join with a mock bias join (see page 38). Press the seams open. Fold in half along the length, WS together, and press.

METHOD

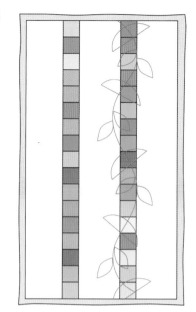

1 Stitch the squares together into two strips with 17 squares in each. Press the seams open.

2 Pin and stitch two white strips to either side of one pieced strip. Press the seams open.

3 Pin the remaining white strip to one side of the second pieced strip. Press the seam open.

4 Join these two pieces to create the overall layout of the quilt top. Press the seam open.

5 Layer and tack/baste with backing and wadding/batting ready to quilt (see page 25).

6 Mark the vine up the centre of one pieced strip, using the straight edge of the curve template to line up with the seam. Flip the template over to alternate the direction to twist the vine. Now add the flowers and the leaves using the templates on page 141. You can offset the curve on the second column if you like (see illustration, right). Repeat on the remaining pieced strip.

7 Over the vines, quilt with big running stitches (i.e. big stitch quilting) in black thread.

8 Once the quilting is complete, remove any tacking/basting and prepare to bind and label. This quilt was bound with the square-cornered method (see page 41).

9 Once the quilt is bound, quilt along each long side ¼in (5mm) from the bound edge.

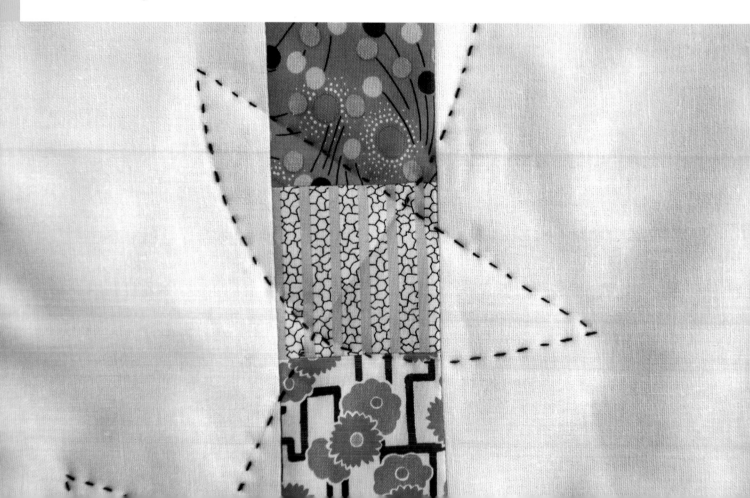

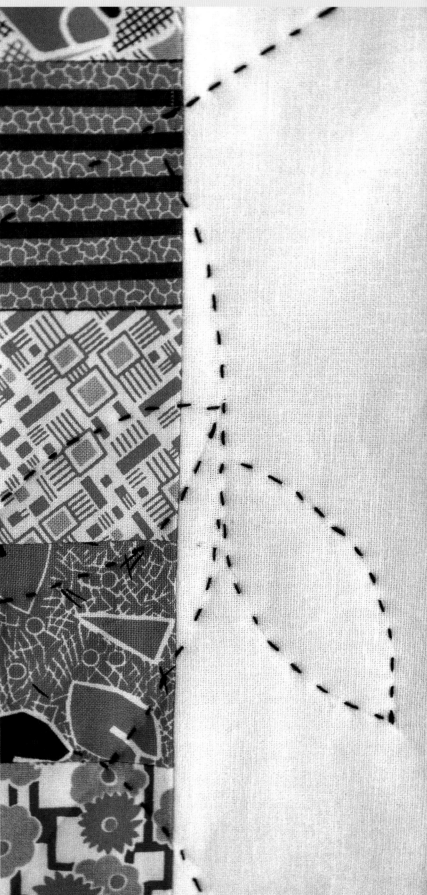

DOLLY quilt

This little quilt uses up lots of scraps and would make a great start to your big stitch journey. Some of the quilting is 'in the ditch', which means it runs along the seams of the pieced blocks. This requires no marking, as the seams do the job for you. The stitching is in the dip, i.e. where the seam is pressed to the left, the stitching will be slightly to the right where there is no SA bulk. Where the quilted diagonal lines cross over blocks with no seams to follow, use your Hera marker or masking tape to mark lines. Use a contrasting colour thread if you want the quilting to make a bolder statement.

MEASUREMENTS

Size: 20½ x 32½in (52 x 82.5cm)

REQUIREMENTS

Fabric scraps: lights, darks and medium tones (see below)

Backing: 25 x 37in (63.5 x 94cm)

Wadding/batting: 25 x 37in (63.5 x 94cm)

Binding: 7½in (20cm) by WoF

Binding: Hera marker or masking tape

Valdani variegated cotton perle no. 12

FABRIC CUTTING

Fabric scraps:

20 square blocks: cut 20 4½in (11.5cm) squares

Four half-square triangle blocks: cut four 4⅞in (12.5cm) squares

Five rectangle blocks: cut ten 2½ x 4½in (6.5 x 11.5cm) rectangles

Five four-patch blocks: cut 20 2½in (6.5cm) squares

Six quarter-square triangle blocks: cut six 5¼in (13.5cm) squares

Binding: cut three strips, 2½in (6.5cm) by WoF. Join to a continuous length with mock bias joins (see page 38). Fold the strip WS together along the length and press.

METHOD

1 Make four half-square triangle blocks (HSTs). Place two of the 4⅞in (12.5cm) squares RS together. Draw a diagonal line from the top-left corner to the bottom-right. Stitch each side of the diagonal line, ¼in (5mm) away. Cut along the drawn line, then open out the patches and press the seams towards the darker fabrics. Repeat to create two more HSTs.

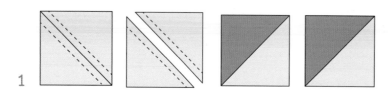

1

2 Make six quarter-square triangle blocks (QSTs). Follow the instructions in step 1 to make six half-square triangles using the 5¼in (13.5cm) squares. Then, pair up a set of HSTs, RS together, lining up the centre seams. Pin to secure. On the back, draw another diagonal line, this time between the two unsewn corners. Stitch ¼in (5mm) each side of this line. Cut along the line and then press the seams open. Repeat for the other two pairs.

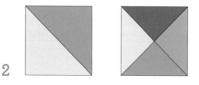

2

3 For the rectangle blocks, stitch the 2½ x 4½in (6.5 x 11.5cm) rectangles together in pairs along the long side, pressing the seams open. Make five.

4 For the four-patch blocks, stitch the 2½in (6.5cm) squares together in pairs. Press the seams open. Stitch the pairs together, to make squares, pressing the seams open. Make five.

5 Arrange the blocks as in the illustration on page 92. Stitch the blocks together in rows. Press the seams in row one to the left and in row two to the right. Continue alternating the seam direction in each row.

6 Stitch the rows together, then press the seams in one direction.

7 Layer and tack/baste the layers ready to quilt (see page 25).

8 The quilt is quilted 'in the ditch' along the vertical and horizontal seams, with diagonal lines following the grid of the patchwork piecing.

9 Remove the tacking/basting and prepare to bind – I bound this quilt with the continuous mitred binding (see pages 39–40). Label the quilt following the advice in the box on page 48.

THE GIFTS

Over the following pages are eleven different gifts. You'll find clear step-by-step instructions and a complete list of the materials and equipment you need for each project. Templates (reproduced actual size) are provided at the back of the book (see pages 138–142), and there are illustrations to help you. Even if you are an absolute beginner, you will be able to tackle all the projects with confidence.

COASTERS

These coasters are a great way to practice a little mindfulness: have a stack ready to quilt when you have a few minutes in your day. A little hand stitching will put you in the zone, and you'll have a useful item at the end of it.

I love the way the circles and partial circles reflect the marks we are trying to protect our surfaces from. There is a thin layer of lining in these, but you could substitute thermal wadding/batting if you want them to be more heat-resistant. I used linen for the fronts as it has a nice texture and is lovely to handle. The backs are scraps of my favourite cotton lawns, giving you a surprise contrast to the fronts. Generally, you can cut eight from a width of craft cotton so I have given the required materials accordingly (see right).

METHOD

1 Follow steps 1–6 of the bagging out method on pages 42–43, sew each front, back and wadding/batting piece together. Turn the coasters RS out and stitch up the opening by hand. Tack/baste around the outside edges to keep them flat.

2 Using a Hera marker, draw around the circle template on the linen, varying its position and the number of circles on each coaster. I tried to keep this very clean and simple – so that the stitching wouldn't seem too heavy.

3 Use big stitch quilting around the outside edge of each coaster, and then follow the lines of the marked circles.

MEASUREMENTS

Size: 4¼in (11cm) square

REQUIREMENTS

Linen: 5in (13cm) by WoF

Backing: 5in (13cm) by WoF

Cotton flannel or very thin wadding/batting: 5in (13cm) by WoF (or substitute for a thermal wadding/batting)

Notions: circle template, 3½in (9cm) diameter (see page 138)

Hera marker

Aurifil 12wt thread

FABRIC CUTTING

Linen: eight 4¾in (12cm) squares

Backing: eight 4¾in (12cm) squares

Wadding/batting: eight 4¾in (12cm) squares

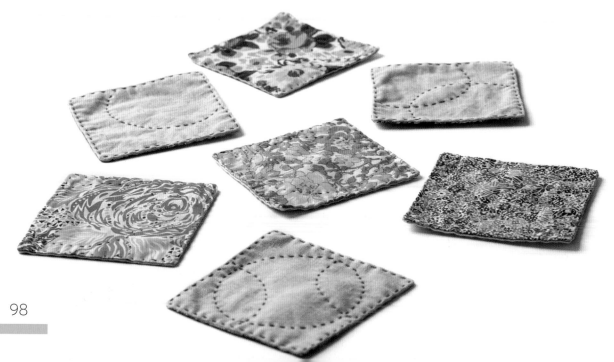

FUROSHIKI cloths

These wrapping cloths originate in Japan, where gifts are often presented wrapped in fabric. This is a great idea for us to adopt as it is environmentally sound, with no unrecyclable wrapping to be disposed of. Traditionally, the recipient of the gift returns the cloth to the gift giver.

Here, I have used a combination of double gauze along with a lightweight lawn to make the cloths double-sided. The layers are held together with big stitch quilting, giving a nod to sashiko stitching but with a less formal interpretation. The combination of fabrics is very easy to handle and great to practise some mindful stitching on. The designs are simple and easy to stitch, but you could easily replace the big stitch with Mennonite tacks, Methodist tacks or running cross stitch, working straight lines across the cloth (see pages 35–37).

MEASUREMENTS

Size: 27 x 20in (69 x 51cm)

REQUIREMENTS

Double gauze or cheesecloth: 27½ x 20½in (70 x 52cm)

Voile or Tana lawn: 27½ x 20½in (70 x 52cm)

Notions: rotary cutting ruler

Hera marker

No. 12 cotton perle – I used the same colour to quilt all three cloths here. On some it contrasts and on others it blends, which gives you a nice idea of the different effects

Optional: spray starch

Circle template: 5in (13cm) in diameter (see page 142).

METHOD

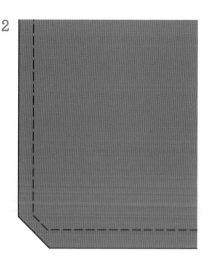

2

1 Place the two fabrics RS together. Pin around the outside edge perpendicular to the raw edge – this will allow you to stitch right up to the pin before removing it and continuing to stitch. The pinning will stabilize the fabrics and keep them together, as the double gauze tends to move a little. You could use a little spray starch, if you want to.

2 Start stitching in the centre of one of the long sides, securing the stitches at the start. Use a ¼in (5mm) SA and stitch around the edge; pay special attention at the corners – sew a couple of diagonal stitches across the corner (see illustration, right). When you reach 2in (5cm) from your starting point, stop and secure the stitches. Snip the seam allowances at the corners. Turn RS out through the sewing gap – pull the furthest corner through the gap first, the rest will easily follow. Slipstitch the opening closed.

3 Roll the outer edge between your fingers (see step 6 on page 43), or use a seam roller, to make a crisp knife-edge finish. Tack/baste in place around the edge, then tack/baste across the diagonals and divide into quarters (see page 25).

4 Quilt all the way around the outside edge, ⅛in (3mm) from the edge. Remove the tacking/basting as you work.

5 Mark your hand-quilting design with your Hera marker (see box, below). Use one of the three designs here or simply mark straight lines in one direction and use Mennonite tacks, Methodist knots or small running cross stitches to hold the layers together.

6 Once quilted, remove the tacking/basting, lightly press and use to wrap your gift. There are many different ways to use the cloth to wrap different gifts, so I encourage you to look up the techniques online.

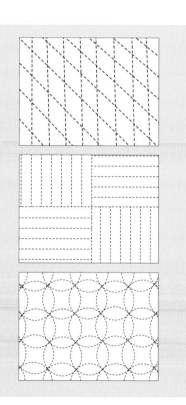

Design one (see page 100)

Mark vertical parallel lines 1½in (4cm) apart, starting from the centre and working to the outside edges. Use the 45-degree marking on the ruler to line up on the edge of the fabric, and mark lines at this angle 1½in (4cm) apart in one direction, to create a diamond pattern.

Design two (see opposite, top)

Mark across the centre in both directions. Fill each quarter with lines 1½in (4cm) apart: two quarters vertical and two quarters horizontal.

Design three (see opposite, bottom)

Using the circle template, start with a circle in the centre of the cloth. Overlap the circle in rows, working out from the centre in all directions, using the spokes on the template to help arrange them (see page 142). This will mean that the design will be balanced on all of the outside edges of the cloth. Quilt in undulating lines from one side to the other of the cloth. There is no need to quilt this in actual circles. These will be formed when all of the lines are complete, and it is easier to work this way.

KITCHEN
table topper

This fun, decorative table topper is right at home in the kitchen. It was inspired by Japanese boromono quilting and uses recycled calico bags – used to hold dried foodstuffs – and a worn-out calico shopping bag. The bags were all washed and the seams unpicked, then laid out to fit like a jigsaw puzzle. Traditionally in boromono, these would have been used to patch a base cloth, and you can work this way too, if you want to. Simply use a second calico shopping bag as a base cloth – you will need fewer small pieces, as it may not need to be completely covered.

Your finished table topper will inevitably look different to mine. If you don't have calico bags, look out for cloth-type printed panels and use these instead. If you are lucky enough to have vintage flour sacks from the 1930s, these would be fun as the backing. The size of my mat was dictated by the size of my calico backing bag, but make yours whatever size works well with what you have to hand.

MEASUREMENTS

Size: 12 x 25in (30.5 x 63.5cm)

REQUIREMENTS

Cotton fabric storage bags: with seams unpicked, washed and pressed

Wadding/batting: 12½ x 25½in (32 x 65cm)

Backing: unbleached calico, 12½ x 25½in (32 x 65cm) OR reuseable calico shopping bag, with sides unpicked, washed and pressed

Notions: repositionable fabric adhesive such as 404 Spray & Fix, a fabric glue stick or Mistyfuse™

Various threads or a variegated perle cotton no. 12

Hera marker

FABRIC CUTTING

If there is something interesting on both sides of a bag, you can always cut it in two to suit your design.

METHOD

1 Place the fabric bags RS up on top of the wadding/batting. If you are using fabric glue, you can dab this onto the WS of the fabric bags when you are happy with the layout. If you want to use Mistyfuse™, cut it to fit the wadding/batting, lay it on top and build up your design on top, ironing to fix everything when you are happy. If you use spray baste, spritz the wadding/batting and then arrange the fabrics, moving them about as needed. The fabric bags need to overlap so that the wadding/batting and glue is not exposed (see illustration below). You can always trim down the fabrics if they overlap too much, or make a patch if there is an exposed area.

1

2 When you are happy with your arrangement, make sure that the fabrics are secured to the wadding/batting. Place the backing fabric RS down on top of the design.

3 Pin around the outside edge, perpendicular to the raw edge. Start stitching in the centre of one of the long sides, securing the stitches at the start. Use a ¼in (5mm) SA and stitch around the edge. Pay special attention at the corners – sew a couple of diagonal stitches across each corner (see step 2, page 42). When you reach 2in (5cm) from your starting point, stop and secure the stitches. Snip away the excess fabric of the seam allowances at the corners, then turn RS out through the gap. Roll the edges between your fingers and thumbs to encourage them to lay flat, then tack/baste in place. Slipstitch the opening closed.

4 Tack/baste the layers together to keep everything stable during the quilting process. Use diagonal lines, then quarters, then lines every 4in (10cm) in both directions to secure (see page 25).

5 Quilt around the outside edge of the mat, taking the tacking/basting out as you go.

6 Next, quilt the different patches. To start with, you may like to mark some straight lines with a ruler and a Hera marker. You don't need to mark every line. Perhaps every 1in (2.5cm). Quilt these and then fill in between them freehand. The areas will be different shapes and the quilting might overlap if you wish. It will also be going in different directions, but make sure that you are quilting all of the raw edges down. You can use different threads for different areas, and perhaps different colours as well as thread types. If you want to keep it more straightforward, use one thread in a variegated colour, as I did, as this will add interest but you won't have to keep changing threads.

7 Continue until the mat is fully covered and then remove the tacking/basting.

SEWING roll

This sturdy sewing roll is bound to become a treasured sewing heirloom. Made from fabric scraps, it is great to use up every last piece of well-loved fabric. The stitch-and-flip stitching of the scraps to the lining and the kantha-style quilting add durability as well as charm.

MEASUREMENTS

Size when open: 5 x 18in (13 x 46cm)

REQUIREMENTS

Fabric scraps/outer sewing roll: at least ten pieces, 6 x 2½in (15.25 x 6.5cm) in size – they need to be slightly wider than the width of the roll, and they will be trimmed down later on. Having the scraps wider allows you to position them at angles, adding interest to the roll

Fabric foundation/inside of sewing roll: 5 x 18in (13 x 46cm) – I used a plain fabric, as the stitches show up well

Wadding/batting: 5 x 18in (13 x 46cm)

Pockets: four 5in (13cm) squares

Pincushion: one 5in (13cm) square

Binding: one fat quarter, 20 x 22in (50 x 55cm)

Notions: card or template plastic, template (see page 138)

Hera marker

Ribbon: ⅜in (1cm) wide, 20in (50cm) long

Button, 1in (2.5cm) diameter

Stuffing for the pincushion

Sewing thread to blend with the lining fabric

Valdani cotton perle no. 12

FABRIC CUTTING

Binding: cut strips 2½in (6.5cm) wide, on the bias. Join together to form a continuous length at least 52in (130cm) long. It needs to go all the way around the roll edge with an overlap to finish. Fold in half along the length, WS together, then press.

METHOD

1 Lay the foundation/lining fabric RS down, then the wadding/batting on top. We will be sewing the strips onto the wadding/batting side. Starting at one end of the roll, lay a strip onto the wadding/batting RS up. This can be straight on or at an angle (see illustration, right).

2 Place a second strip RS together with the first strip, straight or at a slight angle to the first strip, and machine sew them together through the wadding/batting and lining along the top edge (see illustration, right). Flip the top strip over so the RS is facing up and seam press. Each strip you stitch will be stitched and then flipped in this way.

3 Add a third strip. You can angle the strips and vary the width of them as you stitch. Sometimes this will depend on the fabrics you have, but you can make it as quirky or as straight as you like. Press as you work to ensure a neat finish, and trim away any fabric beyond the ¼in (5mm) SA.

4 Continue to cover the entire strip (see illustration, below right). When you reach the top of the strip, trim the edges in line with the wadding/batting and the lining.

5 You can now quilt the roll. I used one colour of thread and quilted parallel to the long sides of the roll, which helps bring a cohesion to the scraps. Start by marking the central line along the length and then 1in (2.5cm) either side. Quilt these lines and then fill the rest in freehand.

6 Make a template of the semi-circle shape (see page 138). At one end of the roll, use the template to mark a semi-circle, and trim to the curve.

7 To make the pockets, on four of the 5in (13cm) squares turn a double hem to the WS of the fabric on one edge. Machine sew along these to secure. These are the top edges of the pockets.

8 From the square end of the roll, measure and mark points at 3in (7.5cm), 5in (13cm) and 7in (18cm) up with pencil lines or a Hera marker. These are the positions of the pockets.

9 Place the first pocket onto the lining fabric RS together at the 7in (18cm) line, with the raw edge in line with the marked line and with the hemmed edge of the pocket towards the bottom of the roll. Stitch the pocket ¼in (5mm) from the raw edge. Flip the pocket so the RS is facing up and the raw edges are in line with the edges of the sewing roll. Pin in place.

10 Repeat for the pockets at the 5in (13cm) then 3in (7.5cm) marks. Place the last pocket in position at the end of the roll, RS up and aligning the raw edges. Pin in place.

11 To make the pincushion, take the 5in (13cm) square and fold it in half RS together. Stitch along the long edge to make a small open-ended tube. Turn RS out. Stitch along one short end, ⅛in (3mm) from the raw edge, with the long seam sitting in the middle. This will be the back of the pincushion and hidden when stitched to the sewing roll.

12 Stuff from the open end until firm, but don't over-stuff as this will distort the roll when finished and make the pincushion harder to stitch in place. Stitch closed ⅛in (3mm) from the raw edge.

1
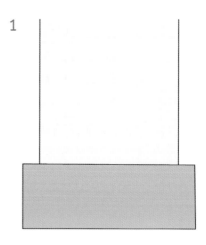

2
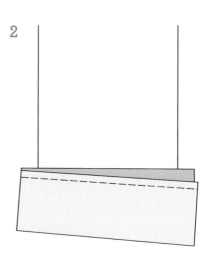

4
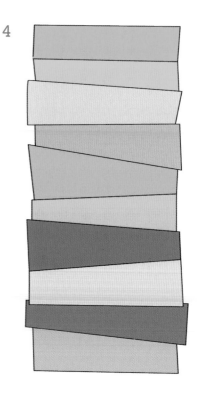

13 Pin the pincushion in place on the sewing roll, about 1in (2.5cm) up from the top pocket, with the seam side of the roll facing the lining fabric, aligning the raw edges. Tack/baste in place (see illustration, right). The stitched ends of the pincushion will be enclosed within the SA when the edges are bound.

14 Start to bind the raw edges of the sewing roll in the centre of one long side. I bound the sewing roll from the outer fabric side. The binding will then be hand finished on the inside of the roll. Use your favourite method; I used a double fold bias binding to give a firm edge and mitred the corners. To end the binding I used a mock bias join to reduce bulk. Finish the binding with slipstitch, securing it to the machine stitching line on the inside of the sewing roll.

15 Pin the centre-point of the ribbon on the outside of the sewing roll, in the centre of the curve. Position the button on top. Stitch the button in place through all of the layers, securing the ribbon at the same time.

13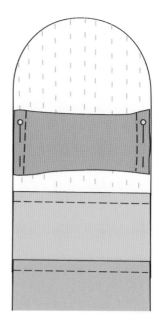

RUBY McKIM
tulip pillow

Ruby McKim was a well-known patchwork quilt designer in the 1930s, who created patterns for a number of newspapers. This wonderful large tulip design is accredited to one of her articles. I have seen a number of quilts from the 1930s that were appliquéd with the stitch boldly prominent and in contrasting black thread. This large tulip, with its bold shapes, works well for this type of technique. Using running stitch along the fold of the fabric is a great way to appliqué. I like the boldness and, depending on your approach, it is a quick way to work, as you don't need to worry about making the stitches invisible.

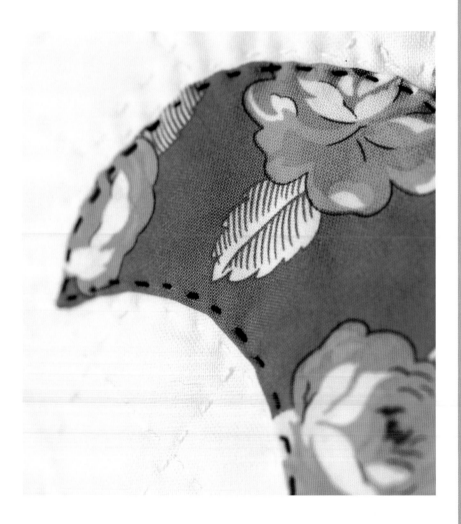

MEASUREMENTS

Size: 18 x 18in (46 x 46cm)

REQUIREMENTS

Appliqué fabrics:

A (navy print): 6 x 9in (15.25 x 23cm)

B/BR (medium blue print): 9 x 9in (23 x 23cm)

C (yellow): 4 x 6in (10 x 15.25cm)

D (green): 6 x 7in (15.25 x 18cm)

E (green): 1¾ x 8in (4.5 x 20.5cm)

Background: 20 x 20in (51 x 51cm)

Wadding/batting: 20 x 20in (51 x 51cm)

Lining: 20 x 20in (51 x 51cm)

Backing: 18in (46cm) by WoF

Binding: 5in (13cm) by WoF

Notions: template card or plastic, templates (see page 139)

Hera marker

Fabric glue stick

Fine sharp pencil

12wt thread, in black and white

Pillow form, 18 x 18in (46 x 46cm)

FABRIC CUTTING

Appliqué shapes:

A x 1, B x 1, BR x 1, C x 2, D x 2, E x 1

Backing: cut two 18 x 14in (46 x 35.5cm) pieces

Binding: cut four strips, 20 x 2½in (51 x 6.5cm). Fold in half along the length, WS together, then press.

METHOD

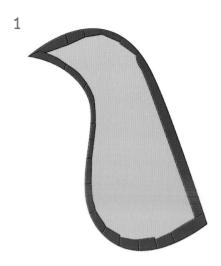

1 If it helps for positioning the pattern pieces, press the background fabric into quarters and then diagonally, or tack/baste along those lines. You can approach the preparation of the appliqué pieces in a number of ways. You might want to mark around the templates on the back of the fabric with a Hera marker – this works best if you rest the fabric on a piece of wadding/batting. Cut out, adding a scant ¼in (5mm) SA. If you don't want to mark the fabric with a crease, draw around the template on the WS of the fabric with a fine, sharp pencil, then cut out, adding the scant ¼in (5mm) SA. Snip into the SA, as this will make the curves sit flatter. Then either press or tack/baste the SA to the WS of the fabric (see illustration, right). I pressed, but equally you could use a glue stick.

2 Place the pieces in position and pin in place. Using black 12wt thread and a big running stitch, appliqué along the edges of the pieces close to the fold. Remember to appliqué down the pieces laying under other pieces first. Remove any tacking/basting and pins as you work.

3 Lay the lining fabric RS down, lay the wadding/batting on top, then finally place the the appliqué cover on top, RS up and centred. Tack/baste together in preparation for quilting (see illustration, right).

4 Mark a grid for quilting 1in (2.5cm) apart. I quilted the background in a white 12wt thread, so as not to fight against the appliqué stitching. First, quilt around the appliqué design, and then quilt the grid.

5 Trim the quilted block to 18in (46cm) square.

6 Prepare the pillow back by folding over a double hem (2in/5cm in total) to the WS on one long side of each backing piece. Stitch to secure – I stitched close to the fold on both edges.

7 Lay the backing pieces on the back of the front panel, WS down. There will be an overlap in the middle. Pin in place around the edges, with the pins perpendicular to the raw edges.

8 Tack/baste around the outside edge, either on the machine or by hand, ⅛in (3mm) in.

9 Use the prepared binding strips to bind the edges using the square cornered binding method (see page 41). Insert a pillow form through the envelope opening on the back of the pillow.

KNOT bag

These traditional Japanese bags, known as *azuma bukuro*, are cleverly made from a rectangle of fabric, which in this case is composed of three squares. They are decorative as well as sturdy. The central square, which becomes the base, needed some reinforcement, so stitching an interfacing in place with Methodist knot stitch is a great solution. Use as many rows as you like – I have overlapped them into the other outer fabrics. I used contrasting thread colours for the stitching to keep the lining in place.

MEASUREMENTS

Size: 13 x 13in (33 x 33cm)

REQUIREMENTS

Outer bag: three 10 x 10in (25.5 x 25.5cm) squares

Lining: 10 x 29in (25.5 x 74cm)

Optional woven sew-in or fusible interfacing: 10 x 12in (25.5 x 30.5cm)

Notions: Hera marker

I used two colours of quilting thread to contrast: Valdani variegated cotton perle no. 12.

METHOD

1 Stitch the three squares for the outer bag together in a row – I used two yellow and one blue, with the blue one in the middle. Press the seams open. To reinforce the blue fabric, which is the base of the bag, place the interfacing in place on the WS. It will overlap the two outer (yellow) fabrics slightly. If you are using a fusible type of wadding/batting, follow the manufacturer's instructions and iron it in place.

2 Using a ruler and Hera marker, starting in the centre of the middle square, mark lines 1in (2.5cm) apart. Use these lines as a guide to stitch the interfacing in place. I have used Methodist knot stitch (see page 36), but you could use Mennonite tacks (page 35) or running cross stitch (page 37) here instead.

3 Now make the strip into the bag. Fold the left-hand yellow square on top of the blue square at the seam, RS together. Stitch along the top outer edge only, starting ¼in (5mm) in from the raw edge, but finishing at the fold with securing stitches (see illustration, right).

4 Fold this yellow square up and out of the way. Fold the right-hand yellow square over the middle blue square, RS together and repeat step 3 to sew the second yellow square to the bottom edge of the blue square (see illustration, right).

5 To make the lining, fold into thirds and press. Place RS up and proceed to sew the seams as in steps 3 and 4 for the outer bag, but leave a 2in (5cm) gap in the middle of one of the seams. Re-fold both pieces to form the characteristic shape of the bag (refer to the photograph on page 116).

6 To line the bag, place the outer bag inside the lining bag, RS facing, and pin along the raw edges. You will be sewing in two parts – sewing one outer yellow piece to its corresponding lining piece at a time. Stitch from the central seam junction, securing the stitches, around the outer edges until you reach the second seam junction. At the point, remember to stitch across the corner with two stitches (see step 2, page 42). Stop and secure the stitches.

7 Now repeat for the second yellow outer piece and corresponding lining. Trim the seam allowances at the points before turning RS out. Slipstitch the gap in the lining closed.

8 Roll the outer edges of the bag so that they lie flat with the lining, tack/baste in place and then big stitch all the way around, ¼in (5mm) from the edge, using the SA as a guide.

9 The bag points knot into a handle for use, and it lies perfectly flat when not in use.

3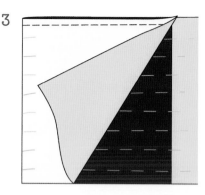

4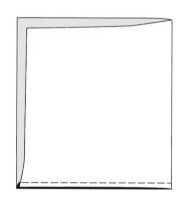

ZOKIN

A zokin is a familiar object in everyday Japanese life, especially for school children. 'Zo' means 'miscellaneous' and 'kin' means 'cloth'. The term itself means 'a cloth for miscellaneous purposes'. At the start of each school year, young children are asked to take in a zokin so that they can help clean their classroom at the end of each day. These cloths can be purchased new or made from old tea towels from the home. They are a good example of fabric always having a part to play in everyday life, and once it is too worn for one task, it can be repurposed for another. These are a great project to get you started on big stitch quilting, as it will not matter if your stitches don't seem perfect in your eyes – you will still have created a useful and decorative household item.

I have used new tea towels here, but you could use old ones, or buy loosely woven fabric (such as muslin or cheesecloth) and cut to the sizes given. I must admit that having a pile of these cleaning cloths waiting to be used makes the tasks in hand more fun knowing that I have stitched them!

MEASUREMENTS

Size: 9½ x 6in (24 x 15.25cm)

REQUIREMENTS

Fabric: use an old (or new) tea towel OR 12 x 19in (30.5 x 48.5cm) of fabric to make two zokin

Notions: Hera marker

No. 12 wt variegated cotton thread

Clover Wonder Clips™, pins or safety pins

FABRIC CUTTING

If you are using a tea towel, remove the hemmed edge on the two short sides of the tea towel - this will make it less bulky when you stitch. Save one hemmed edge if you want to make a hanging loop. One of these cut in half will be enough for both zokin loops

Cut the tea towel in half lengthways - this will make two zokin. If you are using fabric, press it flat and continue from here.

METHOD

1 Fold the half tea towel or fabric: fold the right-hand short end over by about two-thirds of the overall width, then fold the left-hand short edge over so that the raw edges meet.

2 Fold the fabric in half now, enclosing the two short raw edges.

3 If you are using half of one of the trimmed hem edges to make a loop, fold this in half and insert by 1in (2.5cm) into the centre fold of the fabric. Pin in place (see illustration, right).

4 You can use Wonder Clips™ to hold the edges together for the quilting, or use pins or safety pin tacking/basting. I like to stitch all the way around the outside edge first, as then I can quickly remove the pins. I start with a knotted thread and a backstitch. I don't hide the knot, I keep it exposed.

5 You can stitch round the outside once or twice, but pay attention when you reach the loop and stitch it to make sure it stays secure.

6 Once the outside edge is secure you can decide on the design for the centre. I kept my designs quite simple and marked them with a Hera marker. I had some stripes in the tea towels so I used these lines as guides for some of the quilting. Follow some of the ideas here, or create your own. I used variegated thread to add some extra interest!

1
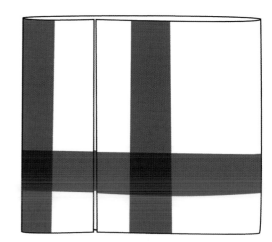

3
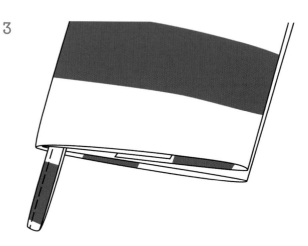

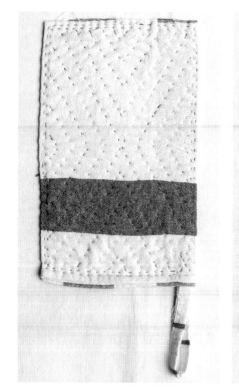

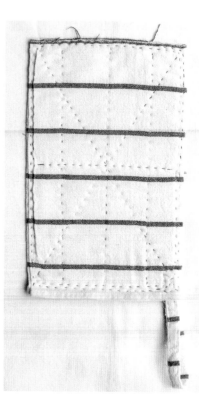

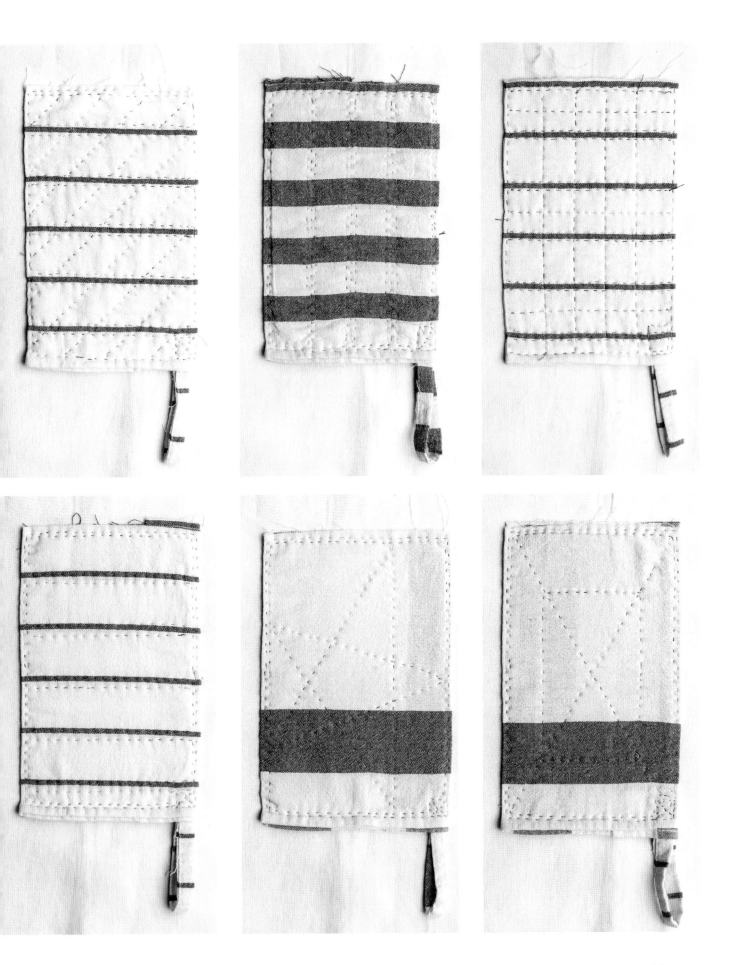

HOT WATER BOTTLE cover

There is nothing more cosy and comforting than a snuggly hot water bottle on a chilly winter's night. This one makes the most of a soft cotton fabric outer, and has lovely simple quilting to hold the three layers together. The Mennonite tack quilting stitch works up really quickly, and copes well with puffy waddings/battings. This textured stitch is worked in alternating directions here, giving added interest.

MEASUREMENTS

Size: 15½ x 10½in (39.5 x 27cm) (this fits a standard hot water bottle, 2-litre capacity, 13 x 8in/33 x 20cm)

REQUIREMENTS

Outer fabric: brushed cotton, cotton flannel, cotton twill or similar, 12in (30cm) by WoF

Lining: quilting or dress-weight cotton, 14in (35cm) by WoF

Wadding/batting: 80 per cent cotton/20 per cent polyester, or a wool type, 14 x 34in (35.5 x 87cm)

Notions: 1in (2.5cm) wide ruler, or any rotary cutting ruler

Hera marker

Variegated cotton perle thread no. 12

Large Clover Wonder Clips™ or pins

FABRIC CUTTING

Outer fabric: 12 x 34in (30.5 x 87cm)

Lining: 14 x 34in (35.5 x 87cm)

Wadding/batting: 14 x 34in (35.5 x 87cm).

METHOD

1 Lay the wadding/batting on a flat surface and put the lining fabric on top, RS up. Now place the outer fabric RS down on top, leaving an equal margin either side.

2 Pin and then machine stitch along both short ends to hold all three layers together (see illustration, right). Put your hand between the lining and the outer fabric and turn RS out. The wadding/batting is now between the outer layers.

3 Roll each sewn edge between your fingers to get a crisp finish and tack/baste along each edge.

4 You can now tack/baste the three layers of the sandwich together. Along the two finished edges use big stitch quilting to secure, removing the tacking/basting as you stitch.

5 On the outer fabric, mark a central line along the length with a ruler and Hera marker. Measure 1in (2.5cm) increments from this line, and mark the entire top with parallel lines.

6 Use these lines to quilt with Mennonite tacks up and down until complete (see illustration, right, and page 35 for how to work this stitch). Remove any tacking/basting. Trim the wadding/batting and lining in line with the outer fabric.

7 With the outer fabric facing you, measure 25in (63.5cm) in from one end and fold the end over. Measuring 10in (25.5cm) from the other end, fold that over on top of the first fold. There will be an overlap in the middle – the hot water bottle cover should be inside out, ready for stitching. Use large Wonder Clips™, or pin along the two edges to secure them.

8 At each corner, measure 2in (5cm) in each direction, and draw diagonal lines from one edge to the other. You will use these lines to shape the corners when you start and stop stitching the sides together.

2

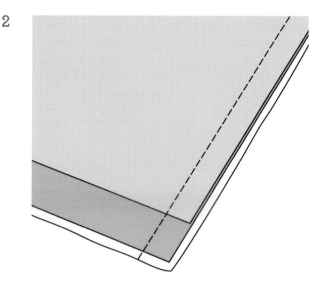

6

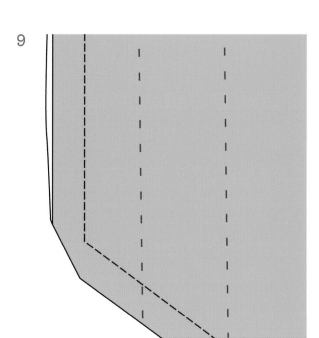

9 Machine stitch, securing the stitches, and starting at one end on the diagonal line. When you get to ½in (1cm) from the raw edge, turn and machine down the side using a ½in (1cm) SA. When you meet the next diagonal line, stitch along that and secure the stitches to finish. Repeat on the other side, then trim the excess from the corners (see illustration, left).

10 Use zigzag or overlock stitch to neaten the raw edges. Turn the cover RS side out, poking out the corners as necessary.

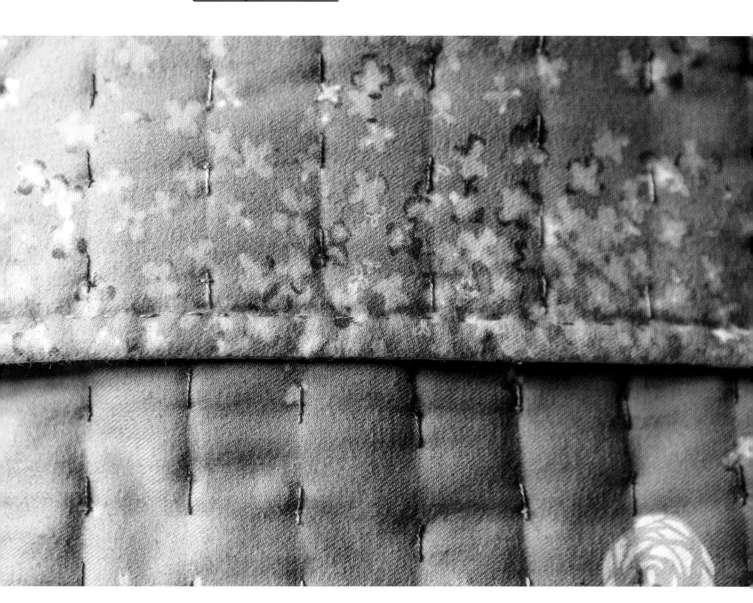

GOLDEN
pincushion

This pincushion truly shows how simple things can work incredibly well. In fact, it is nearly too good for everyday use. In Tokyo, there is a temple where needles are blessed in a ceremony each year; I would take mine in this pincushion.

This little pincushion would also work well with ombre-style prints or shot cotton. Using ombre fabric would mean that you only need one piece of fabric, but you will get different shades of the one colour. Depending on how close these colours run together, you may need to cut individual squares rather than strips, as I did here. If you use a shot cotton, the warp and weft will be different colours. As the light hits the fabric, it will appear to be different colours (another way of making one fabric work really hard for you). As I used linen here, I added fusible interfacing to help stabilize the fabric on the back of the pincushion, as it had quite a lot of movement. Depending on your fabric choice, you may not need to do this.

The opening on the back for stuffing is closed with cross stitch, instead of the more common invisible slipstitch (see the photo on page 131). This is in keeping with the Japanese idea of *wabi-sabi*, where imperfection is something to be celebrated and not hidden.

MEASUREMENTS

Size: 6 x 6in (15.25 x 15.25cm)

REQUIREMENTS

Front: 10in (25.5cm) square

Wadding/batting: 10in (25.5cm) square

Lining: 10in (25.5cm) square

Backing: one fat quarter (20 x 22in/51 x 56cm fabric)

Woven fusible interfacing: 7 x 6½in (18 x 16.5cm)

Notions: stuffing

Cotton perle no. 12

FABRIC CUTTING

Front: cut six 9 x 1½in (23 x 4cm) strips

Interfacing: cut into two 6½ x 3½in (16.5 x 9cm) pieces

Backing: cut two 6½ x 3½in (16.5 x 9cm) pieces.

METHOD

1 Lay out the strips, long sides together (I alternated the direction of mine so that there was variation in colour between them). Stitch the strips together, along their long sides, pressing the seams open.

2 Now cut six strips across the seams, in 1½in (4cm) increments. Reposition the strips to align the newly cut edges and create the grid pattern (again, I alternated the position of every other strip to create a difference in colours). Pin at each seam, perpendicular to the raw edge for the most accuracy. Stitch all of the strips together and press the seams open (see illustration, right).

3 Lay the lining fabric WS up and then the wadding/batting on top. Place the pieced squares RS up centrally on the wadding/batting. Tack/baste together, ready to quilt. Use running cross stitch to hold the layers together, making a stitch at every seam junction (see page 37).

4 Trim the lining and wadding/batting to 6½in (16.5cm) square.

5 Fuse the interfacing (following the manufacturer's instructions) to the WS of the two pieces of backing fabric.

6 Pin the backing pieces RS together along one long side. Stitch taking a ¼in (5mm) SA, leaving a gap of 2in (5cm) in the middle of the seam and securing the stitches each time you start and stop sewing. Press the seam open.

7 Place the backing RS together with the front of the pincushion (see illustration, right). Pin around the outside edges, perpendicular to the raw edge. Stitch all the way round the outside edge, making sure you stitch two stitches across the corners (see step 2, page 42). Remove the pins as you get to them.

8 Trim the points from the corners of the seam allowances. Turn RS out through the opening in the back. Poke out the corners and stuff.

9 To close the opening on the back, I used more cross stitches, close together. Start by hiding the end of the knotted thread in the stuffing. Work a half stitch in one direction, and then work back again, completing the cross. Work across the opening, then knot the thread to finish and pull through into the stuffing. Trim the thread.

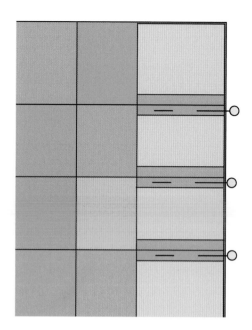

2

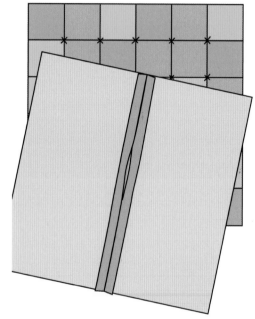

7

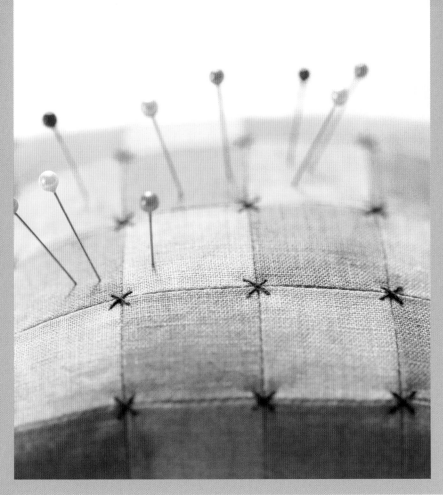

LAVENDER
bags

This is a lovely way to use up small pieces of really precious fabrics, or some that may have become worn. The darned and patched areas can become a decorative feature, and something to show off rather than hide. The darning stitches become a visible part of the process, and stitching the bag opening with the large cross stitches adds to the feel. This very much fits in with the Japanese ethos of *wabi-sabi*, where imperfection (in this case the darned patch and the hole closure) is seen as something to be celebrated.

METHOD

1 The velvet that I used frays, so I neatened the edges of each square with zigzag stitch on the sewing machine before starting. Place your patch wherever you like: you may have fabric to use that has a real hole, and in that case you will want to patch that over. I placed my patches to the side of the square, so that part of it will be in the seam, as I liked the off-centre look. Pin the patch or use a glue stick to keep it in place.

2 Using the perle thread, stitch rows of running stitch over the patch, ¹/₈in (3mm) apart, working backwards and forwards. I extended the stitches into the plain areas of the square. Then work the stitches in the other direction. Some of the stitches will cross over and this is fine.

3 For the loop, fold the ribbon in half and pin it to the top centre of the patched square (the loop will be inside the bag when you stitch it). The ends of the ribbon should extend beyond the raw edge by about 1cm (½in); see the illustration, right.

4 Place the patched square RS together with the backing fabric square. Pin at the corners and perpendicular to the raw edges in the centres of the sides. Leaving a gap in the middle of one side of 1½in (4cm), start by securing the stitches then stitch around the edge, stitching across the corners with two stitches (see step 2, page 42).

5 Trim the excess from the seam allowances at the corners and turn RS out. Spoon in the dried lavender through the gap. About one third full works well.

6 Pin or hold the edges of the opening together and, using the perle cotton, stitch a row of half cross stitches along the edge. Start before the opening and finish after. Then turn the work and stitch back along to complete the cross stitches.

MEASUREMENTS

Size: 4½ x 4½in (11.5 x 11.5cm), plus hanging loop

REQUIREMENTS PER BAG

Front: velvet, 5 x 5in (13 x 13cm)

Back: bark cloth or textured linen fabric, 5 x 5in (13 x 13cm)

Patch of scrap fabric: approximately 2½ x 2½in (6.5 x 6.5cm)

Hanging loop: 10in (25.5cm) of ³/₈in (1cm) wide grosgrain ribbon

Notions: cotton perle no. 12

Dried lavender

Fabric glue stick (optional).

3

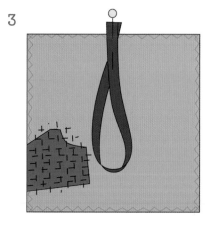

TABLE centre

Big stitch quilting was often used in quickly stitched utility and string quilts in times of need. Every last scrap was used and the quilting was simply designed and quickly executed. This little quilt pays homage to those times, but frames the scraps, giving them pride of place amongst a frame of quilting.

This is a lovely project when you want to use every last piece of a treasured fabric. I've stitched a mini quilt — it can sit on a table or hang on a wall, but equally you could make it into a pillow for a cosy stitching chair. The plain border really accentuates the framed fabrics, and the big stitch quilting adds interest and texture.

MEASUREMENTS

Size: 20 x 20in (51 x 51cm)

REQUIREMENTS

Scrap fabric strips: eight to ten, depending on the width, maximum length 12in (30.5cm)

Border: cotton and linen mix fabric (Essex linen), 9in (23cm) by WoF

Wadding/batting: 20½ x 20½in (52 x 52cm)

Backing: 20½ x 20½in (52 x 52cm)

Non-woven lightweight sew-in interfacing: 6in (15.25cm) square

Notions: cotton perle no. 12

Rotary ruler and Hera marker

Template on page 138

FABRIC CUTTING

Border: two 7½ x 6½in (19 x 16.5cm) pieces and two 7½ x 20½in (19 x 52cm) pieces.

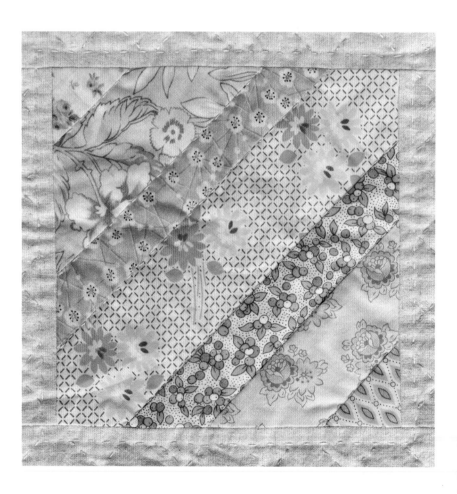

METHOD

1 Start by stitching the scrappy strip centre. Place one strip along the diagonal of the square of interfacing, RS up. Make sure the strip extends over the edges – you will trim back once the square is covered (see illustration, right).

2 Place the second strip RS down on top, aligning the raw edges. Stitch them together from the ends of the strips, not just the edge of the interfacing. Flip the top strip over. Repeat on the other side of the first strip. Press (see illustration, below right).

3 Now add a fourth and fifth strip on each side in the same way and press. Continue until you have covered the foundation square. How many strips you use will depend on their width, so you may not need the same number on each side of the central strip.

4 Square up the finished patchwork from the WS, to a 6½in (16.5cm) square. This may not be the size of the foundation, as this tends to shrink a little as you stitch it.

5 Stitch the small border rectangles to either side of the square. Press the seams towards the border. Stitch the long borders to the remaining two sides. Press as before.

6 Lay the wadding/batting down then place the backing fabric RS up on top. Place the patchwork on top, RS down. Pin in place and use the template at each corner to mark a curve. Cut along this curve through all three layers.

7 Stitch together as for bagging out (see pages 42–43), starting and stopping in the middle of a straight side. You may want to snip the seam allowances of the curves in the corners to help them sit flat, depending on the fabric used. Once turned RS out, stitch up the turning gap. Tack/baste around the outside edge and lightly tack/baste the three layers of the quilt together.

8 Big stitch quilt around the outside edge of the quilt, following the seam edge as a guide. Remove the tacking/basting as you work.

9 Quilt in the ditch on the pieced centre and then all round the edge ¼in (5mm) away from the seam line. Again, the seam allowance is your guide.

10 Mark a diagonal grid over the rest of the table centre with the lines 1in (2.5cm) apart, using your rotary ruler and Hera marker. Quilt with big running stitches to complete.

1

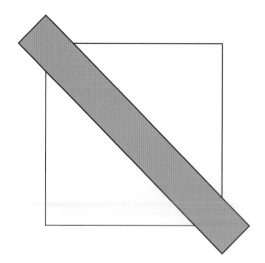

2

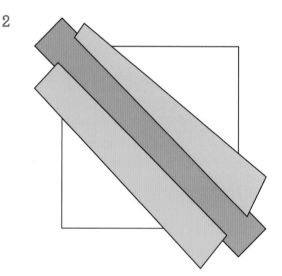

TEMPLATES

All of the templates shown on pages 138–143 are reproduced actual size. Simply copy them onto firm card or template plastic and cut neatly around the outline.

Coasters circle quilting template,
see pages 98–99

Sewing Roll top trimming template,
see pages 108–111 (also used for
the Table Centre on pages 134–137)

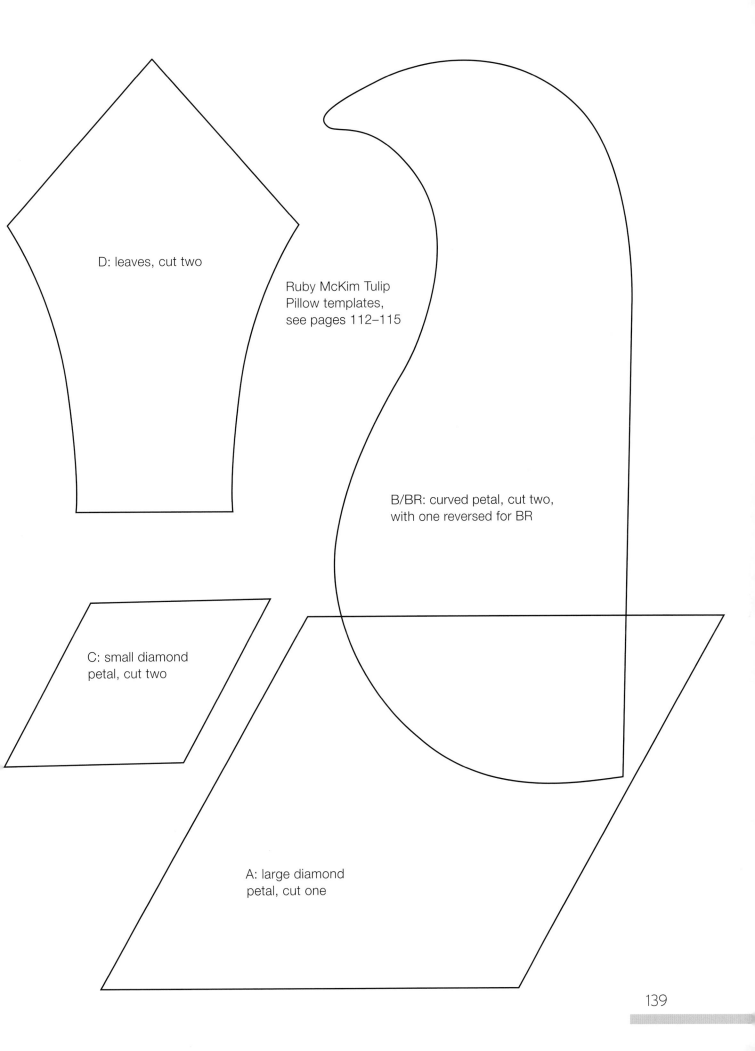

D: leaves, cut two

Ruby McKim Tulip
Pillow templates,
see pages 112–115

B/BR: curved petal, cut two,
with one reversed for BR

C: small diamond
petal, cut two

A: large diamond
petal, cut one

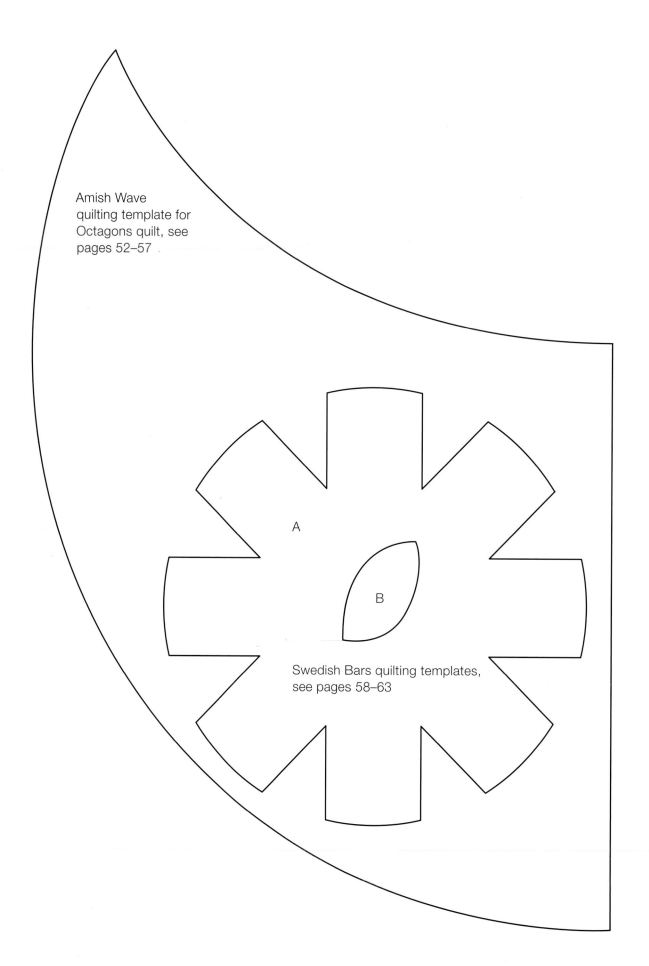

Amish Wave
quilting template for
Octagons quilt, see
pages 52–57

A

B

Swedish Bars quilting templates,
see pages 58–63